SHAKESPEARE

SHAKESPEARE
CONTRASTS AND CONTROVERSIES

KENNETH MUIR

UNIVERSITY OF OKLAHOMA PRESS : NORMAN

Also by Kenneth Muir
(ed., with others) *Shakespeare: Man of the Theater* (Newark, Del., 1983)
(ed., with Stanley Wells) *Aspects of Shakespeare's "Problem Plays": All's Well That Ends Well, Measure for Measure, Troilus and Cressida* (New York, 1982)
(ed., with Stanley Wells) *Aspects of King Lear* (New York, 1982)
(ed.) *Shakespeare: The Winter's Tale* (London, 1981)
Aspects of Hamlet (New York, 1979)
Shakespeare's Comic Sequence (Liverpool, 1979)
The Sources of Shakespeare's Plays (Hartford, Conn., 1978)
The Singularity of Shakespeare and Other Essays (Liverpool, 1977)
Aspects of Macbeth (New York, 1977)
Aspects of Othello (New York, 1977)
Shakespeare's Tragic Sequence (London, 1972)
(with S. Schoenbaum) *New Companion to Shakespeare Studies* (New York, 1971)
Shakespeare, the Comedies: A Collection of Critical Essays (Englewood Cliffs, N.J., 1965)

Library of Congress Cataloging in Publication Data

Muir, Kenneth.
    Shakespeare: contrasts and controversies.

    Includes index.
    1. Shakespeare, William, 1564-1616 — Criticism and interpretations — Addresses, essays, lectures.   I. Title.
PR2976.M746   1985b   822.3'3   85-994
ISBN 0-8061-1940-3

To Roger and Inga-Stina Ewbank

Contents

Preface

This book is a sequel to *The Singularity of Shakespeare*, and, like that, it is a collection of my recent articles on drama. There are three justifications for such a collection: that the articles are not easily accessible, that they throw light on each other and that they develop or clarify previous writings by the author. On the first point, since many of these articles first appeared in *festschriften*, in foreign journals or in conference proceedings, they would certainly be difficult to track down. On the second point, although all twelve were commissioned, I was able to choose interrelated topics, and there are a good many cross-references from one article to another. On the third point, I need only say that as my writings extend over half a century, I have often had second thoughts. I believe, nevertheless, that the book has a unity in diversity and that it illustrates and unites most of my Shakespearian and dramatic interests over the past half century — theatrical, editorial, textual, critical and comparative.

My theatrical interest came first by my proximity to the Old Vic and when, as an undergraduate, I was invited by John Masefield to take the part of Antipholus of Syracuse in his production of *The Comedy of Errors*. He discovered later that he had confused me with a namesake of mine, but too late to eject me from the part. From then until 1974 I acted in many of Shakespeare's plays and directed others by writers ranging from Euripides to Marlowe and from Shakespeare to Chekhov.

It was my interest in drama and an edition of Wyatt's poems which led to an invitation from Una Ellis-Fermor to edit two of the first plays in the revised Arden edition of Shakespeare, *Macbeth* and *King Lear*. I had acted in three separate productions of *Macbeth* and directed *King Lear* (in collaboration with Clare Welch). In another production years later I played the

ix

part of Gloucester. The fact that I had constructed my own texts of *King Lear* and *Troilus and Cressida* for my productions had introduced me to one aspect of editing, and that I was requested to revise my editions of *Macbeth* and *King Lear* after more than thirty years, accounts from my article on the text of *King Lear* in the present volume.

Editing Shakespeare made me realise that although much had been done to establish reliable texts and to elucidate words and phrases, it was still possible to apply to the plays new critical ideas and to widen the study of Shakespeare's sources. I felt, too, that the reaction against Bradley's methods had gone too far — and this was before I was appointed to the chair at Liverpool of which Bradley was the first holder. Shakespeare's method of characterization was a topic which chimed with my theatrical interests, and I have followed up my previous essay on 'The singularity of Shakespeare' with the first chapter in the present book, in which the ideas are developed and clarified.

Shakespeare needs to be seen in relation to his fellow dramatists both in England and abroad; and I have tried to make comparisons, as well as to widen the repertory of the English theatre, by means of actable translations. I followed a version of *Le Misanthrope* (prepared in collaboration with William Melton and performed by the York Settlement Community Players) with a translation of Racine's *Athalie*, made at the request of G. Wilson Knight, who wanted to produce it, along with four other Racine plays, a Corneille and seven comedies of Calderón. The essays on Racine and Calderón in relation to Shakespeare exhibit my continuing interest in this field, together with my conviction of the centrality of Shakespeare's work.

Here, as in previous books and editions, I have touched on stage history, and it will be apparent that I believe that Shakespeare was generally wiser than his interpreters both in the theatre and outside it. Here the moral is simple, however often it is ignored: trust Shakespeare.

Some of the chapters were originally delivered as lectures, and I have retained some of the rhetorical devices designed to influence audiences of different kinds. The opposition between the position taken up in one chapter and another is more apparent than real: it is necessary in different contexts to stress different aspects of the subject. I hope the method of Shakespearian characterization described in Chapter 1 is not contradicted by the didacticism of Chapter 2, and that my questioning of some of Eliot's critical views is compatible with my belief that he is the greatest poet of my time.

I am indebted to many friends and colleagues, particularly to Keith McWatters, Ann L. Mackenzie and J. Leeds Barroll. I am grateful to the Folger Shakespeare Library, which sponsored two of the lectures, to the Cheltenham Arts Festival, who invited me to give the first of their annual Shakespeare lectures, and to the organizers of the conference on *Stendhal et le domaine anglais* (1983).

Kenneth Muir
Liverpool, May 1984

1

Shakespeare's Open Secret

One of the embarrassments of writing about Shakespeare is to discover when one appears in print that, as Hector remarked about Troilus and Paris, one has glozed but superficially on the question at issue. I grew up in the age of Bradley, and like most Shakespearians of my generation, I was later influenced by the criticisms made of his method by Edgar Elmer Stoll, Lily Bess Campbell, Levin Schücking, and L. C. Knights. I came to assume that Bradley read subtleties into the plays which would have astonished an Elizabethan audience or, indeed, the poet himself; that he was too little aware of theatrical considerations; and that, as Knights put it, he did not know that *Macbeth* was more like *The Waste Land* than *A Doll's House*. In fact, as we now know, Bradley was a keen playgoer, and he always believed and asserted that Shakespeare's plays were essentially dramatic poems. Some of the most memorable passages in his *Shakespearean Tragedy* are on a subject he professedly omitted — the poetry of the plays. On the other hand, the most memorable passages of his critics are not those where the plays are considered specifically as dramatic poems but rather those which concentrate on the moral issues raised in them. Leavis's quarrel with Bradley on Othello and Knights's quarrel with him on Hamlet and Macbeth were largely due to their conviction that these tragic heroes were bad men who had been whitewashed by Bradley. He had been seduced by the poetry Shakespeare puts into their mouths, much as some men today are seduced by advertisements which persuade them to buy nicotine and alcohol by associating these slow poisons with attractive and apparently accessible girls.

Some of the criticisms made of Bradley are unjustified. He was fully aware that there was a vital difference between

1

characters in a play and living persons. He pointed out:

> To consider separately the action or the characters of a play ... is
> legitimate and valuable, so long as we remember what we are
> doing. But the true critic in speaking of these apart does not really
> think of them apart; the while, the poetic experience of which
> they are but aspects, is always in his mind; and he is always aiming
> at a richer, truer, more intense repetition of that experience.[1]

Although he sometimes made the mistake of considering
what happened off stage, or before the beginning of the action,
he could never have made the kind of mistake into which
Helen Faucit fell in her letters about Shakespeare's heroines.
When she played Imogen she was convinced that the character
would not long survive after the end of the play:

> Happiness hides for a time injuries which are past healing. The
> blow which was inflicted by the first sentence in that cruel letter
> went to the heart with a too fatal force. Then followed, on this
> crushing blow, the wandering hopeless days and nights, without
> shelter, without food even up to the point of famine. Was this
> delicately nurtured creature one to go through her terrible ordeal
> unscathed? We see that when food and shelter came, they came
> too late. The heart-sickness is upon her: 'I am sick still — heart-
> sick'. Upon this follows the fearful sight of, as she supposes, her
> husband's body. Well may she say that she is 'nothing; or if not,
> nothing to be were better'. When happiness, even such as she had
> never known before, comes to her, it comes, like the food and
> shelter, too late. Tremblingly, gradually, and oh, how reluctantly,
> the hearts to whom that life is so precious will see the sweet smile
> which greets them grow fainter, will hear the loved voice grow
> feebler! The wise physician Cornelius will tax his utmost skill,
> but he will find the hurt is too deep for mortal leech-craft.[2]

Bradley did not read *Hamlet* as though it were *Middlemarch*.
Nor was his aim to give separate character sketches of the
dramatis personae, but rather to encourage people to 'read a
play more or less as if they were actors who had to study all the
parts ... This, carried through a drama, is the right way to read
the dramatist Shakespeare; and the prime requisite here is
therefore a vivid and intent imagination'.[3]

Bradley's weakness, oddly enough, was not that he was a bardolater — though he once remarked that the appreciation of Shakespeare was the whole duty of man — but that he often seems to be apologizing for faults which would not be visible to an audience. He did not fully appreciate that things invisible to an audience should not be regarded as flaws. The performances he witnessed in the later years of the nineteenth century were adaptations, and he never understood that the plays were perfectly designed for the Elizabethan theatre. It may be added that Bradley sometimes invented psychological reasons for actions dictated by the plot, that he ignored the differences between Elizabethan and nineteenth-century psychological theories and that his own theories did not make enough allowance for irrationality.

The situation has, of course, changed during the last seventy-five years. Everyone now agrees that Shakespeare's plays belong primarily to the theatre, and most of us believe that in all his mature plays Shakespeare was professionally as competent as modern directors and wiser than most of his critics. We have had the oppportunity, which Bradley's generation had not, of seeing productions which obeyed, or at least acknowledged, Elizabethan stage conventions. Everyone now knows about unlocalized scenes, the fluid construction of the plays, Shakespeare's scenic art, the use of rhetorical patterns, multiple consciousness, direct self-explanation, the use of imagery and so on. One result of this critical revolution is that we have had to modify our views on Shakespeare's method of characterization. This does not mean that Bradley's method was absolutely wrong, or that Shakespeare was so careless an artist that he cheerfully allowed absurd inconsistencies in characterization — that he created a Macbeth who could not have murdered Duncan, an Othello who could not have developed into a jealous maniac, an Angelo who could never have lusted after a novice.

Bradley provides a useful introduction to the subject of my paper: how far ought we to modify Bradley's method of approach to Shakespeare's characters? To put it in another way, what are the means by which Shakespeare creates characters who seem to be more lifelike that those of other dramatists?

In many ways, of course, Shakespeare's method is not very different from that of Racine, Molière, Chekhov or Ibsen. He, like them, creates credible characters by the actions they are made to perform, by what they say about themselves and others, by what characters, friends and enemies, say about them, by the speech patterns they use, even by their silences. We may choose Hamlet as a convenient example because he is the best known of all Shakespeare's characters. Hamlet feigns madness, spares Claudius, kills Polonius, sends Rosencrantz and Guildenstern to their deaths, grapples with Laertes at Ophelia's grave-side. He laments Gertrude's remarriage, vows to avenge his father's murder, admires an old play about Dido, inveighs against Ophelia, castigates his own delay, praises Horatio's imperturbability, meditates suicide, preaches to Gertrude. He is said by Ophelia to have had a noble mind and to have been the observed of all observers; by Claudius he is said to be a fever in his blood but also most generous and free of all contriving. To Horatio he is 'sweet Prince' and to Fortinbras one who would have made an excellent king. Any interpretation of Hamlet's character would have to take note of these and many other words and actions; but, as he tells us, he is not so easily played upon as a pipe. This is a *reductio ad absurdum* of the old method of character analysis, and no one would now regard it as adequate. If we consider some of its limitations we shall obtain an insight into Shakespeare's own method of creating character.

The main limitation is that such an attempt to pigeon-hole a Shakespeare character evades the ambiguities and ambivalencies which are an essential part of his method — what Maurice Morgann meant by the term 'secret impressions'. Our 'impressions and understanding of a scene may be at variance', and Morgann argued that this was an effect deliberately contrived by the poet and that 'the Principles of this Disagreement are really in human Nature'. He was arguing that we have conflicting impressions about our friends and acquaintances and Shakespeare's realization of this made his characters truer to life — more real — than the characters of other dramatists. Morgann was concerned with the conflicting impressions which are caused by what the characters do and say, and by what others say about them. I want to enlarge the question so as to embrace five or six points that Morgann could ignore in writing on Falstaff.

First, we may consider the expectations of the audience from their previous knowledge of the story and the extent to which Shakespeare fulfilled or disappointed those expectations. This is a matter which is assumed by anyone who writes on Greek tragedy. The plays written by Euripides and Sophocles about Electra derive much of their interest and significance from their deviations from the Aeschylean version; just as, in our own day, Sartre and O'Neill assumed our knowledge of the Oresteia, and Cocteau and Anouilh played on our knowledge of the Oedipus story.

Most of Shakespeare's original audience would have been acquainted with the story of Lear, and they would all expect him to be restored to the throne. When Edmund sends his sword to countermand the death-sentence, most members of the audience must have believed — or at least hoped — that Cordelia would be saved.

Hamlet, to take another example, had been popular for a decade when Shakespeare transformed it. He relied on the fact that the audience would make comparisons. He tantalized the expectations of the audience and teased them into thought. Waldock and other critics have argued that Shakespeare was foolishly pouring new wine into old bottles and that traces of the old motivations, of the old primitive avenger, blatantly conflict with the character of the introspective hero of the new version. The original Hamlet would doubtless have made obscene remarks to Ophelia, spared the King at his prayers so as not to send him to heaven, referred callously to the corpse of Polonius as 'the guts' and murdered his old friends Rosencrantz and Guildenstern without a qualm. But, we are told, the Prince who speaks the great soliloquies or meditates on the special providence in the fall of a sparrow, would never have done such brutal things. *But he did*: Shakespeare deliberately retained some of the characteristics of the old avenger. The conflict between the old avenger and the new — one might almost say between the Old and New Testaments — was one of the ways by which the character of the Prince was made stereo-scopically real. It is not surprising that there have been several hundred interpretations of Hamlet's character, many of them based on the text, or a fraction of it, and therefore plausible.

There may well have been more than one play about Julius Caesar before Shakespeare wrote his. In any case — and this was the reason why Ernest Schanzer called *Julius Caesar* a problem play — Shakespeare could dally with conflicting views on the assassination: whether Brutus and Cassius were martyrs in the cause of freedom, or criminals who deserved to be relegated to the lowest circle of hell alongside Judas.

The story of Coriolanus was also well known, but not previously dramatized. It was frequently used by political theorists to illustrate the evils of democracy: only Machiavelli condemned Coriolanus for his treachery. But Shakespeare could nevertheless set up conflicting impressions about his hero. He does this, more overtly than usual, in a curious speech by Aufidius, who advances a number of different explanations of Coriolanus's banishment:

> I think he'll be to Rome
> As is the osprey to the fish, who takes it
> By sovereignty of nature. First he was
> A noble servant to them, but he could not
> Carry his honours even. Whether 'twas pride,
> Which out of daily fortune ever taints
> The happy man; whether defect of judgement,
> To fail in the disposing of those chances
> Which he was lord of; or whether nature,
> Not to be other than one thing, not moving
> From th'casque to th'cushion, but commanding peace
> Even with the same austerity and garb
> As he controll'd the war; but one of these —
> As he hath spices of them all — not all,
> For I dare so far free him — made him fear'd,
> So hated, and so banish'd. But he has a merit
> To choke it in the utt'rance. So our virtues
> Lie in th'interpretation of the time,
> And power, unto itself most commendable,
> Hath not a tomb so evident as a chair
> T'extol what it hath done.
> (*Coriolanus* IV.vii.33-53)

Aufidius offers several explanations: pride, defect of judgement, trying to apply military discipline to peace-time government. There is some truth in all of them; but as Aufidius has good reason to hate Coriolanus, what he says is not the whole truth. We have to balance it with what his friends and relations say; what the choric figures who prepare the senate house for a meeting conclude about his virtues and defects; and above all we have to consider the subtext of his own speeches, his love for his wife, his fatal devotion to his dreadful mother, his feeling that compromise was the enemy of integrity — this is underlined by his repeated theatrical imagery — and his hatred of the common people, which may be traced to his inadequate upbringing. It has often been pointed out that Valeria's description of the boy Marcius was intended to reflect on the immaturity of his father:

> O' my word, the father's son! I'll swear 'tis a very
> pretty boy. O' my troth, I look'd upon him a
> Wednesday half an hour together; has such a confirmed
> countenance! I saw him run after a gilded butterfly;
> and when he caught it he let it go again, and after
> it again, and over and over he comes, and up again,
> catch'd it again; or whether his fall enrag'd him,
> or how 'twas, he did so set his teeth and tear it.
> O, I warrant, how he mammock'd it!
> (*Coriolanus*, I.iii.57-65)

If one analyses any of Shakespeare's major characters, one soon unveils similar complexities; and Morgann was surely right when he argued that the impression of overwhelming reality given by Shakespeare's characters was due to this. A similar impression of human reality is obtained by Paul Scott in *The Raj Quartet*, in which we get a variety of conflicting impressions of the different characters, according to the viewpoint of the person through whose eyes we see the events. This is rather different from the technique used by Browning in *The Ring and the Book*, for although Browning uses as his spokesmen nine or ten different characters, there is no over-all ambiguity: we never doubt that Pompilia is an innocent and saintly victim and that her husband is a villain.

I turn now to another cause of conflicting impressions: the use of stage types as the basis of a character, though never as simply as the *commedia dell'arte* types in *Love's Labour Lost*. Sometimes, indeed, there is an ingenious fusion of several different types. Falstaff, for example, is based on the *miles gloriosus,* but he is also a Vice or Riot, derived from moralities and interludes — and as such he represents the World, the Flesh and the Devil. Imposed on these is the allegedly hypocritical heretic, Oldcastle, whose characteristics survive in the occasional sactimoniousness displayed by the fat rogue. (It may be added that several critics believe that the character reflects the feelings of the poet in his relationship with the recipient of the Sonnets.) It was appropriate for Morgann to choose Falstaff as his chief exhibit in his essay on Shakespeare's method of characterization, and it is a pity that most commentators on Morgann have concentrated on his paradoxical defence of Falstaff's courage.

The influence of morality plays is more apparent in the tragedies, and it has often been shown that Shakespeare blends the influence of the metaphysical struggle between vice and virtue with a more modern, secular, psychological characterization. Iago is a demi-devil, anxious to bring Othello's soul to damnation; but he is also a character animated by jealousy, colour prejudice, and other very human motives. In addition to this blending of the psychological and the metaphysical, we have to remember (as Muriel Bradbrook reminds us) that Shakespeare was breaking the stereotypes of honest soldier and barbarous Moor. This, which so disgusted Rymer, was yet another way by which Shakespeare played with his audience. Rymer thought that a dishonest soldier was an incredible character: he did not realize that Shakespeare made use of this assumption by making everyone refer to Iago's honesty. An audience, with its inevitably stock responses, would expect a white professional soldier to be a plain blunt man, so that Iago's deviousness, apparent in the opening dialogue with Roderigo, would upset their expectations. In the same way, they would believe that blackness was the devil's colour and that a blackamoor would be cruel, evil and passionate. Shakespeare in the first two acts depicts a Moor who falsifies these expectations.

It would be easy to show that both *Macbeth* and *King Lear* combine the metaphysical with the psychological. I am not, of course, arguing that they are morality plays, but merely that the background of the psychomachia adds a metaphysical dimension to the characters. In *Macbeth* the good and evil supernatural are continually presented, and in *King Lear* the good and evil children are as plainly differentiated as the sheep and goats in the parable. With *King Lear* there is an additional complicating factor. The story was not merely well-known and legendary but archetypal and mythical, so that the audience has the feeling, as it watches the love test in the first scene, or the scene in Act 4 where the proud king and the proud daughter kneel to each other, that they are witnessing, one might almost say *re-enacting*, something that happened 'A great while since, a long long time ago'. Such a feeling is bound to affect, if only subliminally, an audience's reactions to the characters of the play. Lear and Gloucester, Goneril and Regan, are vividly realized characters, with different speech patterns, characters so delusively real that they have attracted the attention of psychoanalysts. On the other hand, they are mythological figures as fated as Oedipus to fulfil their destinies.

Another branch of Shakespeare's art which affects his method of characterization is his use of verse. It is more difficult to differentiate characters in verse than in prose. Shakespeare's triumphs in the plays written at the end of the sixteenth century — Shylock, Beatrice, Falstaff, Rosalind — must have tempted him to abandon verse, as Ibsen did in mid-career, because, as he said, verse had done immense injury to the art of the theatre. Stendhal, earlier in the century, had reached the same conclusion. His reason for preferring Shakespeare to Racine was that blank verse is closer to natural speech than rhymed Alexandrines. English verse, he declared enthusiastically, was able to say everything. The Alexandrine was no more than a *cache-sottise*. He allowed that verse plays gave a great deal of pleasure, but it was not a dramatic pleasure. Audiences enjoyed listening to noble sentiments expressed in beautiful verse — poetry recitals rather than drama. The most precious moments in the theatre were the short moments of perfect illusion; and beautiful verse was the enemy of illusion. What was needed, Stendhal wrote in 1822, was prose tragedy. He quoted Macbeth's words on seeing the ghost of Banquo and asked: 'What verse, what rhythm could add to the beauty of such a sentence? The irony of this question is that the words he quoted were part of a regular line of verse. But he was right to feel that Shakespeare was able to express directly and simply things that were impossible for Racine. If Shakespeare had been born a hundred years later, he could not have used the words to which Dr Johnson objected in Lady Macbeth's invocation of the murdering ministers: 'peep', 'blanket' and 'knife'. To Shakespeare, born in the sixteenth century, nothing was common or unclean.

Yet Stendhal was wrong on several counts. His knowledge of English versification was apparently not enough for him to recognize a line of blank verse; his suspicion of anything poetic and his desire for prose tragedy showed that he appreciated only one part of Shakespeare's quality; and his belief in the supreme importance of illusion ignores the way an audience can believe in the reality of the scene at the same time as it enjoys the poetry. The illusion is never complete except for very naive spectators (such as Partridge in *Tom Jones*) but it is not destroyed or even minimized by the poetry. No one listening to one of Macbeth's or Hamlet's soliloquies thinks primarily of the poetry unless the actor destroys the rhythm or the sense: it is the failure to do justice to the poetry which distracts our attention from the meaning.

In some dramatists, verse does indeed have a levelling effect, so that the style of an old man is no different from that of a young woman. But Shakespeare was careful, after his earliest plays, to alter his style to suit the character speaking. Romeo's initial speeches reveal the artificiality of his love for Rosaline, whereas the equally artificial sonnet he shares with Juliet on their first meeting is a means of revealing a marriage of true minds. In *Hamlet* the rhetorical excess of the Dido speeches throws into relief the colloquial agony of Hamlet's ensuing soliloquy, and the rhymed couplets of *The Mousetrap* (being a stage further away from colloquial speech than the blank verse of most of the play) make us believe that Hamlet is speaking naturally, however poetical his speeches are. Hamlet, indeed, has the most varied styles of any character in the whole of Shakespeare's dramas, and in the theatre we are hardly aware when he moves from prose to verse or from verse to prose.

Since Caroline Spurgeon, Mikhael Morozov and Wolfgang Clemen wrote on the way imagery can be used to differentiate character, it has been generally recognized that even when characters draw their images from the same field, the particular images are appropriate to the characters who speak them. Othello uses sea imagery in a romantic and imaginative way; Iago's use of the same imagery is technical and pedestrian. Othello uses jewel imagery; Iago, like the enterprising monetarist he is, has straightforward references to cash. Troilus and Pandarus both use cooking imagery, but in ways appropriate to their characters.

Imagery therefore provides another of the secret impressions which complicate our conceptions of the characters. The acting imagery used by Coriolanus reveals his revulsion against playing the part assigned to him by the patricians, the imagery used by Leontes when he falls a prey to the green-eyed monster conveys in the most economical way possible the turmoil in his soul, and Viola's image about her imaginary sister reveals something of her own secret passion — though she is far too sensible to pine away.

In the introduction to his translation of *Macbeth*, Maurice Maeterlinck suggested that Shakespeare used imagery to reveal the unconscious mind of his hero; and everyone recognizes that the prudential reasons he advances in the crucial soliloquy in Act 1 Scene 7 against murdering Duncan — universal condemnation, punishment in this life, compelled to drink the poisoned chalice — are all undermined and overturned by the sense of moral horror which the imagery discloses.

One other cause of conflicting impressions is the relationship of a particular play to those which immediately preceded it and, indeed, to the totality of the poet's work and to the themes which occur in play after play. The seed of one play can sometimes be found in one he had written not long before (with which perhaps he was dissatisfied).

Now although Shakespeare was able to identify a wide range of characters, wider than those of any other dramatist, he is more likely to identify with major characters, whether villains or heroes, than with a second sentry or a third citizen; with Angelo, Isabella and Claudio rather than with the Provost. To put it in another way, the reality of Macbeth, or Othello, or Hamlet, is so convincing to us because the poet imagined himself under the skins of those characters. Instinctively he was wondering how he would have felt and what he would have done if he had discovered that his mother had committed adultery with the murderer of his father, what he would have done at Inverness or in Cyprus. I suggest that the presence of the poet as a secret and unacknowledged *dramatis persona* adds another and very potent secret impression to complicate our reactions to the characters. I am reminded by Inga-Stina Ewbank of a letter written by Strindberg about his *Son of a Servant*. He said he had not wished to write a biography or a volume of confessions, but that he had 'used his life, which he knew best of all lives, to try to formulate the history of the growth and development of a mind and to explore the concept of character of which the whole of literature rests'.

In the preface to the second edition of the book, Strindberg referred again to the same question: 'Whether the author has really, as he has at times believed, experimented with viewpoints, or incarnated himself in different personalities, polymerized himself, or whether a gracious providence has experimented with the author, must, for the enlightened reader, emerge from the texts.'

It was natural that Strindberg, simply because he was a dramatist, should speak, even about an avowedly autobiographical work, in such terms. It can be said of Shakespeare too that he experimented with viewpoints, that he incarnated himself in different personalities and that (to paraphrase 'polymerize') he passed through successive variations in his various characters. He would learn from his incarnation in different pesonalities, just as Edgar learnt from the various roles he assumed during the course of the play: Poor Tom, Demoniac, Peasant, Guide, Champion and Future King.

I turn now to a matter which applies not merely to Shakespeare but to all dramatists whose plays are regularly performed. Every new production of a play, whether good or bad, provides a different perspective on it; and, of course, no two performances of the same production can be identical. Let me give some examples from productions of *Troilus and Cressida* in the present century. When Edith Evans played Cressida in 1913, she went all out for comedy. As she took leave of Troilus, she was pinning on her hat, visibly intent on her change of fortunes and bored with his demands that she should be faithful. When the play was staged in 1922 by the Marlowe Society to an audience which included war veterans, it seemed bitterly relevant to those who had been additionally disillusioned by the Treaty of Versailles. When the play was performed in modern dress at the Westminster Theatre at the time of Munich, the war scenes became more interesting than the love scenes. As Desmond McCarthy wrote: 'The interesting result of modernising the play and presenting the characters in contemporary dress — Thersites is a dingy war correspondent (wearing a red tie); Helen and Cressida as cocktail party lovelies etc. — is to bring us straight into contact with the mood in which the play was conceived and written.'[5]

In the days of the Phoney War — the lull before the invasion of France — the play was revived by the Marlowe Society, and the debates in the Greek camp and in Troy were 'followed with a fascinated recognition of the immediate relevance at every point'. There was a revival in Edwardian costume directed by Tyrone Guthrie at the Old Vic, in which the love plot became 'thoughtless undergraduate seduced by bitch'. There have been six revivals at the Memorial Theatre since the first International Shakespeare Conference. In the 1960 revival directed by Peter Hall and John Barton the part of Cressida was taken by Dorothy Tutin, who [we are told] was 'a wisp of rippling carnality that [was] almost unbearably alluring', 'sweltering with concupiscence', 'almost unbearably erotic'. An actress who could so arouse the sexual fantasies of the critics went far to explaining why Troilus found her so enchanting. But this was not the most important thing about the production. The directors showed that the play was 'a planned, architected, coherent and powerful drama, with Hector and Achilles the symbols of a conflict between chivalry and brutal opportunism, to which the ruin of Troilus by the faithless Cressida is secondary'. After more than 350 years the play had come into its own. In later Stratford revivals the play was made more negative and more cynical, so that one critic in 1968 headed her review 'THERSITES WAS RIGHT'. I am not concerned here with determining which production was closest to Shakespeare's conceptions (supposing these could be ascertained) but merely with the effect of the over-all idea of the directors on the way the characters were presented.

We are bound to have our views of characters modified by brilliant performances, even when they run counter to our preconceptions, as (I confess) both Edith Evans's and Dorothy Tutin's Cressida ran counter to mine. But when Sybil Thorndike played Volumnia at the Old Vic and could not conceal her dislike of that creature's opinions, or when Edith Evans delivered Katherine's sermon to the other wives as an ironical attack on male chauvinism, or when Judi Dench as Lady Macbeth seemed literally possessed by the spirits of darkness, we may disagree with these interpretations, but we cannot forget them.

Actors collaborate with dramatists, as the player Shakespeare appreciated. Stanislavsky declared that when an actor speaks Hamlet's soliloquy, 'To be or not to be', he puts into the lines much of his own conception of life:

> Such an artist is not speaking in the person of an imaginary Hamlet. He speaks in his own right as one placed in the circumstances created by the play. The thoughts, feelings, conceptions, reasoning of the author are transformed into his own ... For him it is necessary that the spectators *feel* his inner relationship to what he is saying. They must follow his own creative will and desires.[6]

We may add that most directors and actors will have studied not merely the theatrical traditions of their roles, even when they strike out a new line, but they and many members of the audience will know something, usually too much, indeed, of what the critics have said. Marvin Rosenberg's experiments with ignorant audiences showed that they often expected things to happen differently. More sophisticated audiences may not be fully conscious of what Coleridge, Bradley, Wilson Knight, L. C. Knights and Eleanor Prosser said about Hamlet, of what Bradley, Eliot, and Leavis said about Othello; but these ghosts will haunt us as persistently as the elder Hamlet haunted his son.

What I am arguing is that the conflicting impressions of a character which we get from all the factors I have been discussing — the disparity between source and play, the disparity between what different characters say about each other, the contrast between metaphysical and psychological

motives, the shattering of stereotypes, the complicating effect
of the poetry, the poet's presumed identification with some of
his characters more than with others, the difference between
one production and another, between one actor and another —
these conflicting impressions are the means by which we are
convinced that the characters are *real*, not real people, but
startlingly natural.

Most of these effects were calculated and some were peculiar
to Shakespeare. He must have known that in many of his
dramas he was playing variations on old themes, that different
opinions expressed by various characters would help to convert the subject of them from a flat to a round characters, that
he was modifying or fusing traditional types and that some of
the plays had a metaphysical dimension. When he was at the
height of his power, he had as much delight in depicting an Iago
as an Imogen or, one may add, a Cloten as a Cordelia, or a
Desdemona as a Thersites. Sometimes, no doubt, as with the
character of Iago, he could write from his inner knowledge of a
dramatist's and an actor's psychology.

Shakespeare is the most popular world dramatist because of
his unrivalled powers of characterization, and this power
depends on the methods I have been describing. These
methods run counter to all orthodox prescriptions of drama-
turgy. William Archer, who thought that Elizabethan and
Jacobean dramatists were inferior to Robertson, Pinero,
Galsworthy and Henry Arthur Jones, and wrote a treatise on
play-writing, would have condemned Shakespeare too if he had
had the courage of his convictions. Make certain, the pundits
tell the aspiring playwright, that there is no discrepancy
between your characters and the actions the plot requires them
to perform. When you have worked out your plot, put down
character sketches as a guide to the scenes. Generally speaking,
avoid any inconsistencies of characterization, but if you cannot avoid them, prepare for them and explain them. Give all
your characters an easily recognized and consistent manner of
speech. Never let them speak out of character etc. This is all
very unlike Shakespeare's method. But he knew, as Stendhal
said, that *la vraisemblance* was the enemy of *la vérité*; or, as one
may put it, that naturalism is the enemy of realism.[7]

NOTES

1. A. C. Bradley, 'Poetry for Poetry' Sake, *Oxford Lectures on Poetry* (Macmillan: London, 1909), pp. 16–17.
2. Helen Faucit, *On Some of Shakespeare's Female Characters* (Edinburgh and London, 1885), pp. 278-9.
3. Bradley, *Shakespearean Tragedy* (Macmillan: London, 1904), p.2.
4. Stendhal, *Oeuvres Complètes*, ed. V. del Litto and E. Abravanel (50 vols., Geneva, 1968–74), vol. XXXVII, pp.8, 19, 86, 146.
5. The quotations from reviews of productions will be found in the newspaper cuttings in the library of the Shakespeare Centre, Stratford-upon-Avon. There is an admirable account of the stage history of the play by Jeanne T. Newlin in *Harvard Library Bulletin*, 17 (1969), 353–73.
6. C. Stanislavsky, *An Actor Prepares*, trans. Elizabeth Reynolds Hapgood (1937; Harmondsworth, Penguin, 1967), p. 228.
7. I am not advocating a retreat to Bradley, but an advance from Bradley; but it would be disingenuous to pretend that Shakespeare's inconsistencies always have the effect of convincing us of the truth of his characters. The character of Ajax is a case in point. In some scenes (Act 2 Scene 1, Act 3 Scene 3) he is brainless, illiterate, foolish and vain. In the scene of his combat with Hector (Act 4 Scene 5) he is sensible, sympathetic and courteous. But the first we hear of him — the Jonsonian character sketch spoken by Alexander in the second scene of the play — has no relation to the boorish butt of Thersites's sarcasm, nor to the gentle knight who fights with Hector. This is one of the reasons why critics suspect that *Troilus and Cressida* underwent some rewriting.

2

Shakespeare's Didactic Art

Samuel Johnson — whatever his limitations one of the most honest of critics — lamented in his famous Preface that Shakespeare 'is so much more careful to please than to instruct that he seems to write without any moral purpose'. Johnson was echoing a common eighteenth-century complaint, as Brian Vickers has abundantly demonstrated. In the next century there was a change. Critics in Germany and America, as well as in Victorian England, assumed that Shakespeare did write with a moral purpose, as Moulton's popular book, *The Moral System of Shakespeare,* exemplifies. In the present century critics reacted against what they regarded as a foolish attempt to show that Shakespeare could hold up his head in the company of Tennyson and Longfellow. Shakespeare, they protested, was not didactic. Mackail, for example, the biographer of William Morris (whose political activities he regarded with some suspicion), declared in his British Academy lecture that Shakespeare 'lets morality take care of itself': he depicts virtues and vices, but 'they are neither approved nor condemned, they are only displayed'. Sir Walter Raleigh, one of my predecessors in the King Alfred Chair at Liverpool, spoke of how, in the tragedies, 'Morality is not denied; it is overwhelmed and tossed aside by the inrush of the sea. There is no moral lesson to be read, except accidentally, in any of Shakespeare's tragedies.[1]' Wilson Knight went further. In *Christ and Nietzsche* he asserted that Macbeth goes from strength to strength by 'the breaking of every inhibition binding him to human values':

> Starting with the disrupted, anxious accents of a nervous wreck, he is, poetically, a new man after the first murder, dramatically a more violent one after the second, and philosophically a noble

17

through unrepentant creature of sublime and courageous self-knowledge and superb poetry at the close, when at last an honest and therefore sin-free relation to his world is established.[2]

Is this really true? Although Wilson Knight is perhaps the most impressive living interpreter of Shakespeare, he is also the most erratic. I need hardly say that I disagree completely with his account of the play in this passage.[3] Macbeth is not a nervous wreck at the beginning of the play, and he is completely disrupted after the murder of Duncan, as any speech in the scene would show:

> What hands are here? Ha! they pluck out mine eyes.
> Will all great Neptune's ocean wash this blood
> Clean from my hand? No, this my hand will rather
> The multitudinous seas incarnardine
> Making the green one red
>
> (II.ii.59-63)

He is again disrupted after the murder of Banquo, whether we regard the ghost as real or an hallucination caused by the pangs of conscience. It seems absurd to speak of his sin-free relation to his world in the last act of the play. He has become callous, convinced that life in meaningless, 'a tale told by an idiot', and unable even to feel grief at the death of his wife. 'There would have been a time for such a word'.

What Johnson regarded as a weakness — writing without a moral purpose — is regarded by Raleigh and Knight as a merit. I feel sure, and I am arguing, that both parties are mistaken. The *Scrutiny* critics did not fall into this error, but I believe they fell into errors of their own. Leavis, Knights and Traversi were so convinced of Shakespeare's didactic purpose that they attacked Bradley for covering up the weaknesses of Shakespeare's tragic heroes. Shakespeare, we are assured, exposed the nasty immaturity of Hamlet's behaviour, the romantic delusions of Othello, the wickedness of Macbeth, the sinfulness of Antony. The attacks by Knights on Hamlet in his early essay, 'Prince Hamlet', and by Leavis on Othello read like the speeches of a prosecuting counsel, whereas Shakespeare himself, though displaying those faults of his heroes which bring about their ruin, appears as Poet for the Defence.

Despite my disagreement with the moralizing strain of these critics, and with those who suppose that *Macbeth* was written to warn us that crime does not pay, I believe that Shakespeare's art, particularly in the Histories and Tragedies, was essentially didactic, as Elizabethan critics thought it should be. The best-known statement on the subject is in Sidney's *Defence of Poesy*:[4]

Comedy is an imitation of the common errors of our life, which he representeth in the most ridiculous and scornful sort that may be: so as it is impossible that any beholder can be content to be such a one ... So that the right use of Comedy will, I think, by nobody be blamed; and much less of the high and excellent Tragedy, that openeth the greatest wounds, and sheweth forth the Ulcers that are covered with Tissue, that maketh Kings fear to be Tyrants, and Tyrants manifest their tyrannical humours, that with stirring the affects of Admiration and Comiseration, teacheth the uncertainty of this world, and upon how weak foundations guilden roofs are builded: that maketh us know

Qui scaeptra saevus duro imperio regit,
Timet timentes, metus in authorem redit.

I have elsewhere written of the self-deception indulged in by Elizabethan schoolmasters and critics when arguing about the salutary effects of the comedies of Plautus and Terence, for these do not really teach the schoolboy to eschew the wickedness of the rakish heroes.[5] When the hero of *The Eunuch* adopts that disguise to obtain access to a girl he admires, he rapes her without anyone in the play deploring his deed. The first English translator was hard put to it to extract a suitable moral from the episode, and he makes the desperate suggestion that Terence deserves the credit for not showing the rape on stage.[6] Plautus and Terence are not really didactic dramatists; they are closer to the writers of festive comedy celebrated by C. L. Barber.[7] It is worth mentioning that Horner in *The Country Wife*, a play which moralists frequently deplore, seduces only those women who ask for it.

It may be objected at this point that Sidney's account of the function of tragedy may suit the tragedies of Seneca and his imitators, Garnier and Jodelle, and the yet unwritten plays of the Countess of Pembroke's circle, written by Daniel, Greville and others, but that it clearly has little relation to the plays written for the popular stage. Sidney wrote before the first Elizabethan masterpieces, and when plays came to be written according to his requirements, they were mainly, if not entirely, for reading. Did those who wrote for the public stage take any notice of Aristotelian or Sidneian precepts? They were certainly aware of them. Jonson, as one might expect, had thought about the theory of tragedy, and put the theory into practice in *Sejanus*. Kyd quotes lines from Seneca in *The Spanish Tragedy* and embodies in it many Senecan characteristics. Shakespeare apparently alludes to Sidney's remarks on the unity of time in *The Winter's Tale*. He echoes most of Seneca's plays, usually, but not always, in the translations of Jasper Heywood and others and there is no doubt that he had read Sidney's *Defence of Poesy*. There is an echo of Sidney's version of Menenius's fable in *Coriolanus*, blending it with three or four other versions[8]; he picks up 'ulcers that are covered with tissue', using them for the disease imagery of *Hamlet;* he refers to 'guilty creatures sitting at a play; and the words 'woe or wonder', describing the effect of the tragedy, seem to echo Sidney's 'admiration and comiseration'. All this does not prove that Shakespeare accepted Sidney's views on the didactic function of drama, but the echoes from Sidney, the direct mention of Seneca, the discussion in Act 2 of the function of drama, and in Act 3 of the purpose of acting, suggest that Shakespeare was considering, more seriously than before, the nature of his art.

It is impossible to believe that the dramatists who wrote for the Lord Chamberlain's company never discussed dramatic theory, or that conversations between Shakespeare and Jonson never touched on the interests they had in common. Shakespeare was succeeded by Fletcher as the leading dramatist of the king's players, and he discussed the nature of tragi-comedy. In 1625 Fletcher was succeeded by Massinger. Neither was the kind of dramatist to go against the taste of the public — the comparative failure of *The Faithful Shepherdess* taught Fletcher a lesson; but one of the first plays Massinger wrote after 1625 was *The Roman Actor*, which in the opening scene contrasts the drama with inferior entertainments, and later in the play the hero is given a long and eloquent defence of the moral function of drama, to encourage virtue and discourage vice:[9]

> If to expresse a man sould to his lusts,
> Wasting the treasure of his time and Fortunes
> In wanton dalliance, and to what sad end
> A wretch thats so given over does arrive at;
> Deterring carelesse youth by his example
> From such licentious courses; laying open
> The snares of baudes, and the consuming arts
> Of prodigall strumpets, can deserve reproofe,
> Why are not all your golden principles
> Writ downe by grave philosophers to instruct us
> To chuse faire Vertue for our guide, not pleasure,
> Condemnd unto the fire?

He goes on to show the way in which drama encourages the desire of honour. Philosophers offer cold precepts:

> But does that fire
> The bloud, or swell the veines with emulation
> To be both good, and great, equall to that
> Which is presented in our Theatres?

When they show vice on the stage, it is not to corrupt youth, but rather to turn them against it. The general argument of this speech was probably derived from Heywood's *Apology for Actors*.[10]

Some dramatists, of course, believed that it was impossible to please the many-headed multitude without lowering their standards. In the preface to *Sejanus*, Jonson confessed: 'nor is it needful, or almost possible, in these our times, and to such auditors, to observe the old state and splendour of dramatic poems with preservation of any popular delight'. Shakespeare, a more popular dramatist than Jonson, may have shared some of his doubts about popular taste. A modern biographer (Ivor Brown) compared him with Noël Coward, and it has often been suggested that such titles as *As you Like It* and *What you Will* were deliberately designed to distance the poet's taste from that of his audience. I doubt this, if only because by this time he had trained the Globe patrons to accept that *As I Like*

It and *As You Like it* were synonymous. I doubt equally whether he shared the tastes of that princely amateur, Hamlet, either in his eulogy of the Dido play, in his criticism of the actors, or in his scorn of the groundlings. But, on the other hand, he was not naive enough to believe that murderers would be induced to confess after seeing a play performed, that usurers would repent after seeing *The Merchant of Venice*, that romantic lovers would behave more sensibly after watching *A Midsummer-Night's Dream*, that people would fling away ambition after watching the fall of Wolsey, or even that usurers, lovers, and ambitious prelates would be deterred by the odium aroused by the dramatist. Justice Gardiner would have remained a scoundrel even if he had seen Shakespeare's depiction of Justice Shallow.[11]

Eighteenth-century critics who complained of Shakespeare's lack of moral purpose or of his failure to satisfy the demands of poetic justice, really wanted him to rig the evidence so as to prove that the world was providentially governed, that the good were successful and the bad unsuccessful. Edmund Blunden's poem, 'Report on Experience', gives the lie to such cosy metaphysics:

> I have been young, and now am not too old;
> And I have seen the righteous forsaken,
> His health, his honour and his quality taken.
> This is not what we were formerly told.

Thomas Rymer, contemplating with horror and disgust the tragic loading of Othello's bed, asked indignantly, 'If this be our end, what boots it to be virtuous?' It is difficult to name a single good tragedy which would satisfy Rymer's demands.

Some critics, indeed, have actually praised Shakespeare for falsifying reality. There is a drinking-fountain in the market square at Stratford-upon-Avon, which bears an inscription from an essay by Washington Irving, written when he paid a visit to the town: 'Praised be the Bard, who gilds the harsh realities of life with innocent illusions'. It is hard to imagine a more absurd misunderstanding of Shakespeare's tragedies. The 'innocent illusions' do not prevent the mad Titus from serving up to Tamora as a *pièce de rèsistance* her wicked sons baked in a pie; they do not prevent Juliet from regaining consciousness five minutes too late; they do not prevent the death of Hamlet from a rapier unbated and envenomed, or the murder of Macduff's family, the drowning of Ophelia, the gouging out of Gloucester's eyes, the ingratitude of Timon's friends; and if Lear is given some innocent illusions when he looks forward to life in prison with Cordelia, they are short-lived:

> Come, let's away to prison.
> We two alone will sing like larks in the cage,
> When thou dost ask me blessing, I'll kneel down
> And ask of thee forgiveness. So we'll live,
> And pray and sing and tell old tales, and laugh
> At gilded butterflies, and hear poor rogues
> Talk of court news, and we'll talk with them too —
> Who loses and who wins, who's in, who's out —
> And take upon's the mystery of things
> As if we were god's spies. And we'll wear out
> In a walled prison packs and sects of great ones
> That ebb and flow by the moon.
>
> (*King Lear,* V.iii.7-19)

When Lear re-enters we know that the pipe-dream has been shattered. He is reduced to inarticulate grief: 'Howl, howl howl!' Many other illusions are destroyed in the course of the play. So much so, that in editing the play Johnson could not bear until then to re-read the last act, preferring Tate's sentimental ending, with the restoration of the King and the marriage of Edgar and Cordelia. More recent critics have imagined a happy sequel, left unwritten, in which Lear and Cordelia are reunited in heaven.

Shakespeare's refusal to give us easy answers is one way of confuting those critics who assure us that his plays are not didactic. For any literature that tells the truth, that exposes illusions, that reminds us that deeds have consequences, has, whether designed or not, a didactic effect on its readers and on its audience.

We should be careful to distinguish between the short-term immediate lessons and the more profound revelations of some aspect of truth. This was a distinction implied by Shelley when he asserted that didactic poetry was his abhorrence. It may well be that Shakespeare was attracted to the story of Lear because it illustrated the dangers of a divided kingdom at a time when James I was advocating the union of England and Scotland, and his choice of the Macbeth story was doubtless motivated by the King's interest in witchcraft and his belief that he was descended from Banquo. Yet few readers and fewer critics would assert that these are the real themes, or the most important themes, of *King Lear* and Macbeth. King Lear is concerned with mightier matters. The King is bidden to renounce love, as Freud put it, 'and make friends with the necessity of dying'. It is also a profound examination of the injustices of society and of man's inhumanity to man; an enquiry into the nature of man, and what unaccommodated man really is; whether the world is providentially governed, and if it is not, should this affect the principles and the behaviour by which we regulate our lives? We emerge from a performance knowing that it is better to be Cordelia than Goneril and Regan — and it would be better even if the wicked sisters had survived — better to be the credulous Edgar than his cleverer brother, better to be Kent than Oswald, better to be Cornwall's rebellious servant than his master — whatever the disasters which overtake the good. Rymer's idea that one can be virtuous only from fear of hell or from hope of prosperity in this life or the next is a cheap and degrading assumption. But it should be added that all the evil characters in the play are destroyed as well as Cordelia, for Shakespeare knew that the will to power is self-destructive. Marlowe, despite his notorious opinions, knew it too.

In one of the best books on the play, *King Lear and the Gods*, William Elton argues that Shakespeare was deliberately ambiguous, so that he could appeal on two levels. The ordinary spectator would assume that the failure of pagan gods to answer prayers or protect the innocent was only to be expected, whereas the more sophisticated spectator in the first decade of the seventeenth century, when the new philosophy called all in doubt, would find reflected in the play his own scepticism and doubts about the workings of providence. It may be so, but we should remember that two of the plays written just before *King Lear* (*Hamlet* and *Measure for*

Measure) and the tragedy written soon after (*Macbeth*) are all set in the Christian era, and in all three Shakespeare goes out of his way to stress the fact, from the lines about Christmas in the first scene of *Hamlet* to the flights of angels mentioned in the last; from Isabella's Christian plea to Angelo for her brother's life, to her forgiveness of Angelo at the end of the play; from the emphasis on Duncan's Christian virtues, 'so meek, so clear in his great office', to the saintliness of Edward the Confessor. The old play of King Leir, moreover, was equally Christian, and Shakespeare's transferring it to pagan times must have been deliberate. He would have learned from Holinshed and Spenser that Leir reigned many years before Cymbeline, and that that monarch's chief title to fame was that Jesus was born during his reign. The older playwright's anachronism would not have bothered Shakespeare, if he had not realised the advantages of a pagan setting. It gave him a much greater freedom, enabling him to ask some fundamental questions without falling foul of censorship. He was, we may say, conducting a kind of experiment, imagining a society in which its more sensitive members are tested to the limit, and who stumble towards the Christian ethic, although they are deprived of the Christian hope. In only one passage is there a reference to a life after death, when Lear, recovering from madness, thinks that Cordelia is a soul in bliss, while he is 'bound upon a wheel of fire'. But this is forgotten in the last scene of the play.

Shakespeare's hypothesis for the purposes of the play neither confirms nor denies his own religious position. In some ways it reflects the profound pessimism of many Christian writers, not merely because they believed that the saving remnant was very small, but because they thought that the righteous suffered their hell in their life on earth.[12] Yet Shakespeare must have felt that if they were to be amply compensated in heaven, they were taking part in a tragi-comedy. If he had written the play during his last period, Shakespeare might have decided on a happy ending, but in 1604-5 he was not in the mood.[13]

I am not suggesting that the plays of Shakespeare's final period represent a turning away from reality — 'gilding the harsh realities of life with innocent illusions' — but their way of facing reality is manifestly different. In tragedy there are no second chances. Although it has been argued that Macbeth has many opportunities to repent, and that even at the end he has the chance of redeeming himself by agreeing to be a caged monster, it is obvious that such an act was only theoretically possible.[14] Macbeth long before had taken the primrose road to the everlasting bonfire. But in tragi-comedy the heroes are given second chances. Leontes, for example, orders the murder of Polixenes, puts Hermione on trial for her life and orders the exposure of Perdita. The child survives to become the bride of Polixenes' son, and Leontes is reunited to the wife he and the audience thought was dead. The story is absurd, 'like an old tale', as we are reminded more than once. But Mamillius is dead, and Hermione is wrinkled. What permits the happy ending is the knowledge that Leontes' jealousy was more like the onset of a disease than a sin, and that he has suffered many years of remorse and repentance and been forgiven by the people he has wronged.

In *Cymbeline* the happy ending depends even more obviously on the repentence of the hero. His murderous rage is caused by apparent proof of Imogen's adultery, but even though he still believes her to be guilty, he repents of ordering her death and admits that she is morally his superior. He seeks death in battle as a punishment for his sin. At the end, pardon is the word for all. Imogen forgives her husband, Posthumus forgives the guiltier Iachimo, and the Roman prisoners are re-preived. Once again the plot is engagingly absurd. Johnson complained of its imbecility, the folly of the fiction in which Shakespeare blended historical material from Holinshed, a tale from Boccaccio, a folk-tale motif, something from a pastoral and the direct intervention of Jupiter. But this curious mixture is subordinated to what seems an obsession with the necessity of forgiveness.

The Tempest centres on the act of forgiveness. Although Prospero has brought his enemies to the island to arrange a marriage between Miranda and Ferdinand, the audience is soon made aware that he is still bitterly angry with the brother who has betrayed him. The purpose of one of his spectacular shows — the enchanted banquet and the appearance of Ariel as a harpy to denounce the three men of sin — is to frighten them into heart-sorrow; and when, at the prompting of Ariel,

Prospero decides to forgive, there is an important proviso:

> Hast thou, which art but air, a touch, a feeling
> Of their afflictions, and shall not myself,
> One of their kind, that relish all as sharply
> Passion as they, be kindlier moved than thou art?
> Though with their high wrongs I am struck to th'quick,
> Yet with my nobler reason 'gainst my fury
> Do I take part; the rarer action is
> In virtue than in vengeance; *they being penitent*,
> The sole drift of my purpose doth extend
> Not a frown further.
> (The Tempest, V.i.21-30).

It is Ariel's prompting that makes Prospero re-affirm his previous intention of forgiving his enemies, and he expresses his determination in words borrowed from Florio's Montaigne.[15] He forgives not because it is a Christian duty but because it is a the rarer action, because he is too proud to do otherwise. It is in accordance with Senecan precepts. The proviso I have mentioned is contained in the words 'they being penitent'. A few minutes later he discovers that of the three men of sin, only Alonso is penitent. Sebastian, when he realizes that Prospero knows of the plot to murder Alonso, says 'The devil speaks in him'; and as for Antonio, Prospero calls him 'most wicked sir, whom to call brother, would even infect my mouth', but he forgives all his faults, in the sense that he will not exact punishment. Caliban, also forgiven, promises to be wise hereafter and seek for grace. Antonio and Sebastian seem to have no remorse and, characteristically, are harsher to Stephano and Trinculo than either Prospero or Alonso.

It is left to the epilogue to put forgiveness in the same context as in that of the last plays. Prospero addresses the audience on behalf of the actors, the dramatist, and of his dramatic role, asking for forgiveness for all three, since he has forgiven his enemies:

> Now I want
> Spirits to enforce, art to enchant;
> And my ending is despair

> Unless I be relieved by prayer,
> Which pierces so that it assaults
> Mercy itself, and frees all faults,
> As you from crimes would pardon'd be,
> Let your indulgence set me free.
>
> (*The Tempest*, Ep. 13-20)

Critics have often sought to minimize the significance of this speech by pointing out that its primary function is to win applause. Yet the play as a whole, when considered in relation to its immediate predecessors, is clearly didactic in intention. If one compares Fletcher's *Philaster* with *Cymbeline*, written in rivalry, we may suppose, with similarities of plot and structure, one is immediately struck with a difference of seriousness. Fletcher never attempts to make anyone wiser or better, whereas Shakespeare, using similar materials, teaches while he delights. Indeed, the fantastic, improbable plays of the last period call attention to their didactic purpose by their very preposterousness. They are designed, in Auden's phrase, to teach people to unlearn hatred and to learn love.

I suggested earlier that to tell the truth about the human condition was itself a moral act, and sometimes a very difficult one. At first sight the tragi-comedies may seem to represent a shrinking from this kind of truth-telling, whether because of the inferior taste of the wealthier Blackfriars patrons or because Shakespeare was exhausted by writing the great sequence of plays from *Julius Caesar* to *Coriolanus*, in which the comedies are as searing as the tragedies. Yet the plays of his final period, although further from naturalism, are still concerned with questions of human nature, questions of right and wrong, and ultimately they are attempts to answer in a secular way the age-old question, 'What must we do to be saved?'

Now most people will agree that there is at least a didactic element in the plays we have been discussing, and they would concede that there is an equally didactic element in the English histories, but it may be more difficult to regard the pure comedies as didactic. Are we not in danger of adopting the pedantic attitude of Holofernes or the humourless stance of Malvolio? Are they not for the most part what C. L. Barber called them, festive comedies, plays that give us a carnival feeling, including even, as Lamb claimed in his apologia for Congreve and Wycherley, a holiday from our consciences? The objection is sound, and it is not fully answered by the element of satire — of Jaques' melancholy, of Malvolio's pomposity, of Dogberry's malapropisms, of Sir Andrew's foolishness, of the badness of Quince's troop of actors, of the pageant of the Nine Worthies. Nor can the convenient conversions of the usurping Duke and Orlando's wicked brother serve the same purpose as the conversions of Leontes, Posthumus and Iachimo.

In the first scene of *A Midsummer-Night's Dream*, Hermia and Lysander lament that the course of true love never did run smooth. Love comedies, after the overcoming of assorted obstacles, end with marriage bells. The dramatist can contrive a plausible postponement of the final happiness by various expedients — infidelity of one of the lovers, parental disapproval, misunderstanding caused by slander, and the confusions caused by disguise. But the mere procrastination of felicity is not in itself an ideal comic formula, and several dramatists use the period of postponement in a more significant way: the lovers are under probation. I have elsewhere attempted to show how this idea can be applied to a number of dramatists — Congreve, Calderón, Marivaux, as well as Shakespeare.[16] The lovers in Congreve's masterpiece, for example, are testing each other. Apart from the fact that Millamant will lose half her dowry if she marries without her aunt's consent, Mirabel wishes to find out whether her outrageous affectations and coquettishness are a true index of her character, or whether they are the armour she uses to protect her genuine sensibility and true love. Millamant for her part wishes to find out whether Mirabel, who is no longer in love with Mrs Fainall, will cease to love Millamant immediately after the consummation of their marriage. She does not wish to dwindle into a wife.

A similar kind of testing may be seen in most of Shakespeare's love-comedies. In *Love's Labour Lost* the courtiers have to expiate their broken vows (to forswear the company of women) and also the foolishness that led them to make such a promise. Proteus has to expiate his jilting of Julia, his betrayal of Valentine and his attempted rape of Silvia, and it must be admitted that most critics find his repentance somewhat perfunctory. Bassanio undergoes a triple test: he has to show, by choosing the right casket, that he is not a fortune-hunter, that he is a true friend by hastening to Antonio's trial on his wedding day and that he has a right sense of values by giving away the ring. The ring is a symbol of fidelity which is never in question, and ingratitude is a worse fault than a broken promise of this kind. Rosalind wants to discover whether the handsome wrestler and bad poet is genuinely in love with her, and whether he is worthy of her love. In the course of the play he displays modesty and compassion, bravery and good sense; he rejects the cynicism of Jaques and saves the brother who had tried to kill him. Viola cures Orsino of his sentimental passion for Olivia, and cures Olivia of her sentimental feelings of her dead brother; and she knows she has succeeded with Orsino when he proves to be more jealous of his page than of his mistress. Isabella is tested three times: by Angelo's sexual blackmail, by the temptation to agree to Claudio's pleading and by the temptation in the last scene not to intercede for Angelo. But in most of Shakespeare's comedies it is the heroine who tests the man, rather than the other way round: it is the heroine who represents sanity.

Some of Shakespeare's lovers need to be re-educated. Beatrice, a more civilized shrew than Katherine, has to be tamed; and Benedick suffers from vanity and self-sufficiency. Both lovers, moreover, are deluded about their own feelings, not realizing that their bickering is a subconscious sign of love. The plotters who bring them together think that it will need a miracle, because they are as deceived as the lovers themselves. Bertram is the least amiable hero in all Shakespeare's comedies, with the possible exception of Proteus; yet Proteus's actions are caused by a kind of love, whereas Bertram's are caused merely by self-love. He is intolerably proud and snobbish, a hopeless judge of character, a betrayer of his own aristocratic standards, a would-be seducer, a liar, and a slanderer of the chaste Diana. Helena performs the apparently impossible task of getting pregnant by him and attempts the even more impossible task of turning him into a tolerable husband. It is only her entrance in the last scene which lifts the suspicion that he has murdered her. He promises to love her 'ever, ever dearly'; and presumably we are meant to entertain the possibility that the marriage will prove to be satisfactory. Lest the male members of the audience should preen themselves on their superiority to Bertram, the choric lords in Act 4 comment on his disgraceful morals:

> Now, God delay our rebellion! As we are ourselves, what things we are! ... The web of our life is of a mingled yarn, good and ill together; our virtues would be proud if our faults whipp'd them not, and our crimes would despair if they were not cherish'd by our virtues.
>
> *(All's Well that Ends Well,* IV.iii.18ff).

In this play, and in *Measure for Measure* and *Troilus and Cressida*, Shakespeare seems to be more conscious than in his earlier plays of man's natural depravity.[17] At least in these so-called problem plays he was being deliberately didactic; and if it is agreed that the testing of love and the rejection of its surrogates — sentimentality and lust — are desirable objects, then we may claim that his love comedies, however festive, have a didactic element, and one that is not merely accidental.

The continuing conviction that Shakespeare's plays are not didactic is due partly to attempts to attach inappropriate morals to them. When Morley retitled *Antony and Cleopatra* as *All for Lust, or the World Ill Lost* (parodying Dryden's *All for Love, or The World Well Lost*), he was judging the protagonists from the standpoint of Rome; he was ignoring the dramatic effect of Cleopatra's ritual suicide and going against the poetic effect of the play as a whole. Bernard Shaw, although he condemned the play in the preface to *Three Plays for Puritans*, did not make this mistake. He thought that Shakespeare in the last act:

> finally strains all his huge command of rhetoric and stage pathos to give a theatrical sublimity to the wretched end of the business, and to persuade foolish spectators that the world was well lost by the twain.[18]

I have confined my attention to Shakespeare's plays, but it would be possible to show that any of the greater Elizabethan dramatists, and many of the lesser ones, assumed that drama ought to be didactic as well as entertaining. Even though we may disagree with Marlowe's opinions, and may even feel some disparity between his table talk and the overt morals of *Doctor Faustus* and *Edward II*, we need not doubt that he had a didactic purpose.

Critics are apt to suppose that the views of the dramatists, even Shakespeare's, were circumscribed by the general opinions of the age, and particularly by the collective opinions of their audience. Of course it is absurd to imagine that all members of an audience thought alike, any more than they do in the modern theatre, or that the dramatists carefully adopted the views of the majority. Two plays about second marriages will illustrate the difficulties involved — *The Widow's Tears* and *The Duchess of Malfi*. It would not be difficult to quote sermons and tracts condemning second marriages, except for dynastic reasons, and it is easy to show that Chapman's two heroines are satirized for their lust and infidelity. One marries again because she hears exaggerated stories of the hero's sexual prowess; the other, who has vowed never to marry again, proposing to starve herself to death in her husband's supposed tomb, is induced to break her vow by her husband who has returned, disguised as a soldier, to test her fidelity. But our sympathies are more with the wife than with the husband, who is criticized by the *raisoneur* for his absurd jealousy and possessiveness; so that the play as a whole seems not to condemn second marriages in themselves, but even to admit that it is perfectly natural for young widows to wish to marry again.

This is more obvious in Webster's play. Although in the main source of *The Duchess of Malfi* it is stated that she married for lust, Webster makes it clear that although she married beneath her, she married for love. Lisa Jardine seems to me both to misinterpret the play and to misjudge the probable reactions of the original audience: 'In the moment of disobeying her brothers and remarrying... the Duchess... is metamorphosed from ideal mirror of virtue... into lascivious whore'.[19] Jardine assumes that Webster agreed with this verdict and that the audience, however much they might pity the heroine in her sufferings, would regard her fate as only to be expected. Even more stangely, Jardine thinks that the audience would have agreed with the views expressed by Ferdinand and the Cardinal. But Webster makes it perfectly plain that both brothers are insanely proud of their blood, that the lecherous Cardinal murders his mistress, that Ferdinand is incestuously in love with his sister, and that he afterwards goes mad. Indeed, he is madly jealous earlier in the play. It is surely impossible to believe that Webster meant us to agree with his ravings:

> I would have their bodies
> Burnt in a coal-pit, with the ventage stopp'd,
> That their curs'd smoke might not ascend to Heaven:
> Or dip the sheets they lie in, in pitch or sulphur,
> Wrap them in't, and then light them like a match:
> Or else to boile their bastard to a cullisse,
> And give't his lecherous father, to renew
> The sin of his back.
>
> (*The Duchess of Malfi*, II.v.87-94)

Thomas Middleton, perhaps a greater dramatist than Webster, may seem in his citizen comedies to be innocent of any didactic intention, but this is merely appearance.[20] In his major plays he exposes the ulcers that are covered with tissue — the hypocrisy of the three main characters in *More Dissemblers Besides Women*, lust in *The Changeling* and *Women Beware Women*. One of the most puzzling pronouncements in Eliot's essay on Middleton is the statement that 'he has no message, he is merely a great recorder'. Certainly he is not didactic in the same way as the author of *The Cocktail Party*, but his message is only too plain.[21] The corruption of society in *Women Beware Women*, revealed not merely by the fact that the central character, Livia, owes her position to her success as a pander, but also by the behaviour of all the main characters, is generally recognized by the critics. Middleton is not merely recording evil, but holding it up to our disapproval. The possessiveness of Leantio and his subsequent fall into the position of being Livia's kept lover, the incestuous passion of Hippolito, the sordidly arranged marriage between Isabella and the half-witted Ward, and the murderous tyranny of the Duke are all exposed and condemned. The same thing is true of *The Changeling*. It could even be argued that in both plays Middleton made the moral too explicit. I am thinking of the last scene of *The Changeling* (for which, however, Rowley was mainly responsible) and the two interventions of the Cardinal in *Women Beware Women*. Webster, Middleton and Ford seem to have felt constrained to point the morals of their plays. Shakespeare knew that it was more effective to let the facts speak for themselves, and that truth-telling was the didactic art in which he excelled.

NOTES

1. *Shakespeare* (Macmillan: London, 1907), p. 196.
2. G. Wilson Knight, *Christ and Nietzsche* (Staples: London, 1948), p. 85.
3. See my edition of *Macbeth* (Methuen: London, 1951, 1984).
4. Philip Sidney, *Defence of Poesy* in *Works* ed. A. Feuillerat (Cambridge, 1923), III.23.
5. Kenneth Muir, *Shakespeare's Comic Sequence* (Liverpool University Press, 1979) Chapter 1.
6. R. Bernard, *Terence in English* (1598).
7. C. L. Barber, *Shakespeare's Festive Comedy* (Princeton, 1959). Cf. Erich Segal, *Roman Laughter* (Harvard University Press, Cambridge, Mass., 1968.)
8. Kenneth Muir, 'Menenius's Fable', *Notes and Queries* (1953), pp. 240-2.
9. Philip Massinger, *The Roman Actor* in *The Plays and Poems*, ed. Edwards and Gibson, III (Oxford, 1976), (I.iii.56-67).
10. Ed. J. P. Collier (1841), p. 21. Notes by Edwards and Gibson.
11. Leslie Hotson, *Shakespeare versus Shallow* (Nonesuch Press: London, 1931).
12. Henry Smith, cited by Kenneth Myrick in *Shakespeare 1564-1964*, ed. E. A. Bloom (Brown University Press: Providence, 1964), p. 61.
13. The alterations in *King Lear* published in the First Folio may have been made then, as Gary Taylor has argued in *The Division of the Kingdoms* ed. Gary Gaylor and Michael Warren (Oxford, 1983).
14. G. R. Elliott, *Dramatic Providence in 'Macbeth'* (Princeton, 1958).

15. Eleanor Prosser, 'Shakespeare, Montaigne, and the Rarer Action', *Shakespeare Studies*, I (1965), p. 261.
16. In a *festschrift* for Eugene Waith (1984).
17. 'Shakespeare and Original Sin', in *Essays and Studies* (Jadavpur University: Calcutta, 1981), p. 9.
18. *Prefaces* (Constable: London, 1934), p. 716.
19. Lisa Jardine, *Still Harping on Daughters* (Harvester Press: Sussex, 1983), p. 77.
20. R. B. Parker, "Middleton's Experiments with Comedy and Judgement', *Jacobean Theatre*, ed. J. R. Brown and B. Harris (Arnold: London, 1960).
21. See Chapter 12 below.

3

Folklore and Shakespeare

In a recent number of the *Mississippi Folklore Register* (X, 1976), which was devoted to Shakespeare, there was a useful bibliography compiled by Philip C. Kolin, containing nearly 300 items. I came across this after I had prepared this lecture and I was slightly embarrassed to discover that I had read less than a hundred of these. If therefore you find me mentioning things which you have seen elsewhere, I hope you will ascribe this to the fact that I had too little time to track down the remaining 200 items in the bibliography.

Folklore now covers a multitude of fields, any one of which could keep one busy for a lifetime — folktales in many languages, proverbial wisdom, folk-plays, witches, ghosts, fairies, seasonal festivals, anthropology, flora and fauna, magic, sports and pastimes, popular medicine, jest-books, totem and tabu, even religious ritual, both pagan and Christian. It stretches from *The Golden Bough* to Freud and Jung.

If one reads the pioneering book by Thistleton Dyer, published nearly a century ago,[1] or the recent book by Roy Palmer on *The Folklore of Warwickshire*[2] (which includes incidents from the reign of Elizabeth II as well as Elizabeth I), one will be convinced that anyone brought up in Stratford-upon-Avon in the middle of the sixteenth century would have come into contact with a wide variety of folk customs and superstitions. What is also clear is that any dramatist writing in the last two decades of the sixteenth century could rely on his audience being equally familiar with the same body of material.

Even entertainments written for the court or the aristocracy could make use of folklore, in the knowledge that it would be understood. I am thinking of such things as the Herne the Hunter scene in *The Merry Wives of Windsor* or the sheepshearing feast in *The Winter's Tale* performed before Princess Elizabeth and her betrothed, or the account of the wet summer in *A Midsummer-Night's Dream*:

> The fold stands empty in the drowned field,
> And crows are fatted with the murrion flock;
> The nine men's morris is filled up with mud,
> And the quaint mazes in the wanton green
> For lack of tread, are undistinguishable.

If one reads the notes in any good edition of Shakespeare, one must be struck by the fact that there is hardly a play which does not have allusions to some branch of folklore, from the legend of the Baker's Daughter, the hobby-horse and St. Valentine's Day in *Hamlet* to the Whitsun Pastorals in *The Winter's Tale*. Shakespeare, moreover, makes use of many folktale motifs, such as the story of the three caskets in *The Merchant of Venice*, the three daughters in *King Lear* and the love-test which was told about many other personages, the good outlaws in *As You Like It* and the wicked stepmother in *Cymbeline*.

This does not mean that the dramatists necessarily believed in the superstitions they made use of for dramatic purposes or that they lamented, as Richard Corbet did, the departure of the Fairies:

> Farewell, rewards and Fairies,
>   Good housewives now may say,
> For now foul sluts in dairies
>   Do fare as well as they.

Two of the books which Shakespeare is known to have read are *The Discovery of Witchcraft* by Reginald Scot and *A Declaration of Egregious Popishe Impostures* by Samuel Harsnett — two sceptical books about witchcraft and exorcism. It may be supposed that the poet, who had a good grammar school education and must have been above average intelligence, was unlikely to have been taken in by the kind of superstition derided by Harsnett:

How were our children, old women and maids afraid to cross a

churchyard, or a three-way leet, or to go for spoons into the
kitchen without a candle? and no marvel. First, because the devil
comes from a smoky black house... with ugly horns on his head,
fire in his mouth, a cow's tail in his breech, eyes like a bason, fangs
like a dog, claws like a bear, a skin like a nigger, and a voice roaring
like a lion; then bo! or oh! in the dark was enough to make their
hair stand upright. And if that the bowl of curds and cream were
not duly set out for Robin Goodfellow the friar and Sisse the
dairy-maid to meet at *hinch-pinch and laugh not*, when the good
wife was abed, why then, either the pottage was burnt next day in
the pot, or the cheese would not curdle, or the butter would not
come, or the ale in the vat would never have good head. But if a
Peter-penny, or a houzle-egg were behind, or a patch of tythe
unpaid to the Church... then ware you walk for fear of bull-
beggars, spirits, witches, urchins, elves, hags, fairies, satyrs, pans,
fauns, sylvans, Kit with the candlestick, tritons, dwarfs, giants,
imps... the mare, the man in the oak... the fire-drake, the puck-
le, Tom Thumb, hobgoblin, Tomtumbler, Boneless and the
rest: and what girl, boy, or old wizard would be so hardy to stop
over the threshold in the night for an half-penny worth of mustard
amongst this frightful crew.

We cannot be certain about Shakespeare's views, for James
I was one of many learned and inteligent people who fervently
believed in demonology.

Here I do not propose to discuss Shakespeare's use of
folktale motifs but rather his method of combining literary
and folk material. It is not always easy to distinguish between
the two kinds of source: obviously a literary source may be
based on folklore. The good outlaws in Lodge's *Rosalynde*,
derived partly from Robin Hood stories, were used by Shakespeare in *As You Like It*, and Imogen's wicked stepmother,
who resembles the Queen in the story of Snow White — the
seven dwarfs being metamorphosed into Imogen's princely
brothers — is put in a story from Holinshead's *Chronicles* and
fused with an old play, *The Rare Triumphs of Love and
Fortune*, and a tale from the *Decameron*.

We may begin with Shakespeare's treatment of the supernatural. There are ghosts in *Richard III, Julius Caesar, Hamlet*
and *Macbeth*. It is obvious that the ghosts who appear to
Richard III and Richmond on the eve of the battle of Bos-

worth have no real connection with the ghosts of popular superstition. They prophesy Richard's defeat and Richmond's triumph, but neither sleeper awakes until the ghosts have vanished, and both men assume they have been dreaming. Shakespeare intends the audience to make the same assumption. The ghosts merely symbolize Richard's sense of guilt and exemplify the timorous dreams of which his wife had spoken earlier.

The Ghost of Banquo is more complicated. It appears twice immediately after Macbeth has mentioned his name. It is not seen by anyone else and Lady Macbeth says scornfully:

> When all is done
> You look but on a stool.

It is clearly an hallucination. Despite the stage direction in the First Folio, which doubtless reflects the practice in Shakespeare's day, it would probably be best for the ghost not to appear at all. This view is supported by the contrast between Macbeth's two descriptions. In the first, suggested by the twenty trenched gashes described by the First Murderer, Macbeth refers to the apparition's gory looks. On the second appearance, his imagination has moved away from the immediate present to the future, when the corpse will be changed:

> Thy bones are marrowless, thy blood is cold,
> Thou hast no speculation in those eyes
> Which thou dost glare with.

The last appearance of the Ghost in *Hamlet* in the closet scene is invisible to Gertrude. It has been suggested that this is because her adultery has made her unworthy to behold her husband's spirit, but the words uttered by him are merely the echo of Hamlet's self-criticism, his 'almost blunted purpose' after having spared Claudius at his prayers. Even the Ghost's words about Gertrude are a reflection of Hamlet's attempt to persuade her to repent.

The appearances of the Ghost in Act 1 are more complex and ambiguous, as many critics have recognized. They reflect the divergent views of Shakespeare's contemporaries about ghosts — namely that it was genuinely the ghost of Hamlet's father, presumably, come from purgatory, where the foul crimes done in his lifetime are burnt and purged away, or that it was the devil in the shape of Hamlet's father:

> The devil hath power
> To assume a pleasing shape, yea and perhaps,
> Out of my weakness and my melancholy
> ... Abuses me to damn me;

or, thirdly, that the ghost was an illusion. Horatio holds the sceptical view at first — 'Tush, tush, 'twill not appear' — but though he goes on to address the Ghost as 'illusion', he is soon converted to the belief that it has an objective existence, because he goes on to ask if it has some foreknowledge of some danger to the state, or if it has returned to reveal the whereabouts of some buried treasure or because it wants something to be done so that he can rest in peace. It disappears at cockcrow, when:

> Th' extravagant and erring spirit hies
> To his confine.

Marcellus then refers to the legend that on Christmas Eve:

> no spirit can walk abroad:
> The nights are wholesome; then no planets strike,
> No fairy takes, nor witch hath power to charm,
> So hallowed and so gracious is the time.

The mingling of theological controversy and the curiosities of folk belief are both apparent in this scene. The ambiguities continue when Hamlet confronts the Ghost:

> Be thou a spirit of health or goblin damned,
> Bring with thee airs from heaven, or blasts from hell,
> Be thy intents wicked or charitable.

Horatio is afraid that the apparition will assume some other horrible form and drive Hamlet mad. After the Ghost has told his tale, it speaks from below the stage and lends colour to the idea that it is the devil in disguise. Here Shakespeare is making use of stage tradition as well as folklore. But few would agree with Eleanor Prosser that the Ghost is indeed the devil. In the long speech which reveals Claudius' crime and Gertrude's adultery, he enjoins Hamlet not to contrive anything against her — 'leave her to heaven' and the pricks of conscience. The Ghost is most perturbed at being murdered:

> Unhousled, Disappointed, Unannealed,
> No reckoning made, but sent to my account
> With all my imperfections on my head.

But Shakespeare has imposed on Catholic ideas of purgatory some quite different associations. In the first place, as the late J.C. Maxwell pointed out, the Ghost comes not merely from another world but from the grave. Hamlet asks:

> tell
> Why thy canonized bones, hearsed in death,
> Have burst their cerements; why the sepulchre
> Where we saw the quietly inurned
> Hath oped his ponderous and marble jaws
> To cast thee up again!

He is not so much a ghost in the ordinary sense of the word as a dead corpse, like the zombies in Haiti who are said to work in the cane-fields. It fits in with other references in Shakespeare's plays. The Duke in *Measure for Measure* tells Isabella that if she were to plead for Angelo's life, her brother's ghost 'his paved bed would break'; Leontes thinks that if he were to remarry, Hermione's sainted spirit would again possess her corpse, and Puck says that with the dawn damned spirits have returned to their wormy beds — not to hell — and at midnight:

> the graves, all gaping wide,
> Every one lets forth his sprite
> In the church-way paths to glide.

Here Shakespeare departs from theological assumptions to make use of common superstition. As Roy Battenhouse puts it, Shakespeare maintains a pagan character for the ghost in *Hamlet*, 'but one deceptively embellished with some super-

stitious touches of nominal Christianity.' The ordinary ghost
in Elizabethan drama was a spirit who came not from the grave
but from a half-classical, half-Christian underworld. As R. H.
West observes, Shakespeare's 'dramatic purpose required a
confusion of pneumatological dogma.' His idea of Hades was
derived partly from memories of Kyd's *Spanish Tragedy* — the
Elizabethan play closest in plot to *Hamlet* — and partly from
the Induction in *A Mirror for Magistrates* in which Sackville
had described:

> the horror and the hell,
> The large great kingdoms and the dreadful reign
> Of Pluto in his throne where he did dwell.
> The wide waste places and the hugy plain,
> The wailings, shrieks, and sundry sorts of pain,
> The sighs, the sobs, the deep and deadly groan
> . . . .
> A thousand sorts of sorrow here, that wailed
> With sighs and tears, sobs, shrieks, and all yfere,
> That oh, alas, it was a hell to hear.

Kyd's Ghost of Andrea likewise describes the deepest hell —
probably derived from Virgil and the *Thyestes* of Seneca (both
of which Shakespeare had read):

> Where bloody furies shake their whips of steel
> And poor Ixion turns an endless wheel
> . . . .
> And murderers groan with never-killing wounds,
> And perjured wights scalded in boiling lead
> And all foul sins with torments overwhelmed.

What I am suggesting is that the Ghost in *Hamlet* is an
amalgam of literary and folklore elements. The description by
the ghost of his prison-house seems more appropriate to hell
than purgatory, and it has been pointed out that spirits would
not (for such a reason) be released from purgatory, that he
speaks of his foul crimes and that he urges Hamlet to avenge
his death. It was dramatically necessary to set up these conflicting impressions which Maurice Morgann thought were a

sign of Shakespeare's supremacy as a dramatist. Is the Ghost Hamlet's father or the devil? Is it an honest ghost? Does he demand revenge or justice? Should Hamlet obey or refuse? The interfusion of theology with classical lore and folklore was essential to Shakespeare's purpose — to arouse in Hamlet's mind and in ours the maximum bewilderment between conflicting ideas as to the right course of action.

When we turn to Shakespeare's treatment of fairies we find the same combination of folklore and literature — but here modified by sheer invention. In nearly all the references to fairies outside *A Midsummer-Night's Dream* Shakespeare seems to conform to popular views — that they were beautiful creatures and not much smaller than human beings. This can be seen in *The Merry Wives of Windsor* in which the bogus fairies who torment Falstaff include Ann Page and Parson Evans[3]; Antony speaks of Cleopatra as a great fairy, a beautiful enchantress. Pericles asks Marina if she was a fairy. One of Imogen's brothers says she is like a fairy; Venus proposes to entertain Adonis by tripping on the green like a fairy. None of these characters is at all diminutive in size, except possibly Ann Page. Venus appears to be larger than Adonis — some say much larger — and Cleopatra is tall enough to exchange clothes with Antony. In *Hamlet* and *The Comedy of Errors* there are references to the fairies' power of enchantment. These fairies are all in accordance with popular ideas. But in two plays we meet a very different sort of creature. If, as most critics believe, *Romeo and Juliet* was written just before *A Midsummer-Night's Dream,* Mercutio's account of Queen Mab, the fairies' midwife, appears to be the place where Shakespeare broke with tradition. For Queen Mab is a fairy looked at through the wrong end of a telescope — she is the size of an agate, her waggon-spokes are made of spiders' legs, her waggoner a gnat, her chariot a hazel-nut.

In *A Midsummer-Night's Dream* as Ernest Schanzer pointed out, there are three irreconcilable sorts of fairies.

Oberon and Titania are of traditional size. Titania, as her name suggests, is no pigmy, and she is large enough to embrace a donkey. Oberon is accused of being the lover of the Amazonian Hippolita, and he retaliates by accusing Titania of being Theseus' lover. In *Huon of Bordeaux* Oberon is some ti.ee feet in height, but he seems taller in Shakespeare's play.

On the other hand, Titania's retainers, Moth, Cobweb, and Mustardseed (as their names suggest) are as tiny as the fairies described by Mercutio. They can hide in acorn cups, wear coats made of mouse-skins, and get tapers from bees. Katharine Briggs has pointed to a number of stories of non-literary origin in which there were tiny fairies. Elidorus, for example, was taken to a fairy kingdom where horses were the size of hares, and Welsh fairies were reputed to dance on rushes and to hide in foxgloves. As Professor Harold Brooks suggests in his excellent edition of *A Midsummer-Night's Dream*, Shakespeare may have heard of these Welsh legends from the boy who played Lady Mortimer in *Henry VI Part 1*.[1]

Puck is different again, the only character who is entirely traditional. He is the Pouke of folklore, Robin Goodfellow and Lob. There are many place names in Warwickshire which refer to Lob or Hob — Hob's Hole, Great Hobbs' Meadow, Hobbin's Close, Hob Ridge, Hob's Moat etc. He is described on his first appearance by one of Titania's entourage:

> Are not you he
> That frights the maidens of the villagery,
> Skim milk, and sometimes labour in the quern,
> And bootless make the breathless housewife churn?
> Those that Hobgoblin call you, and sweet Puck,
> You do their work, and they shall have good luck.

Shakespeare, it has been said, has fused an earth-demon with a house-fairy. He confesses that he loves crude practical jokes: he likes things to fall out preposterously. The portrait would be recognized by any of Shakespeare's acquaintances at Ilmington or Shottery, and no doubt by many Londoners as well. Fairies, you will recall, were supposed to punish sluts and reward those who were clean and tidy.

Oberon was mentioned in the first instalment of *The Faerie Queene* and he is a kind of choric figure in Greene's *James IV*, two works with which Shakespeare was familiar. There is a reference by Robert Greene to a play about the King of Fairies, and one was performed in 1593. The most intriguing source, however, is to be found in *The Merchant's Tale* of Chaucer. There, Pluto and Proserpine, who are called by Chaucer the King and Queen of the Fairies, have a prolonged argument on the relative immorality of the two sexes. Pluto vows to give back old January's sight if May cuckolds him, and Proserpine vows that she will enable May to evade the accusation. January helps his wife to climb a pear tree where her lover is waiting, and at the very moment when they flagrantly embrace, the husband's sight is restored. Here, as in *A Midsummer-Night's Dream*, there is a quarrel between the King and Queen of the Fairies, and the recovery of the sight of mortals through supernatural agency.

Oberon and Titania come partly from medieval romance, partly from classical mythology and partly from the theory that they were pagan deities who had survived into the Christian era. The name Titania comes, of course, from Ovid, who connects her with Diana and Lucina, the goddess of childbirth, which is why Titania is so concerned with the welfare of the child of her votaress.

James I in his *Daemonology* describes one kind of spirits:

> which by the Gentiles was called Diana and her wandering Court and amongst us was called the Phairie.

The King of the Fairies was often identified with the god of the underworld, even by those who had no knowledge of classical mythology. This supports the theory that fairy-lore was connected with the persistence of pagan rites in medieval times. As Dr. Vlasopolos has recently shown, St. John's Day, the Christian counterpart of the summer solstice celebration, is inseparable from the pagan midsummer night. It is characterized by the exorcism of evil spirits and follows immediately the license and misrule of the previous night. It is the only holy day celebrating the nativity rather than the death of a saint, and this relates it to the theme of procreation. It was therefore appropriate for a play performed on a wedding day, as *A Midsummer-Night's Dream* originally was.

The substitution of one child for another was thought to be an activity of fairies, and one which explained the presence of ESN children in normal households. So the quarrel between

Oberon and Titania is about a changeling stolen from an Indian King, although Titania's own story is quite different — that the child's mother, a votaress of her order, had died in childbirth. (So Diana in *Pericles* watches over the fortunes of Thaisa and her daughter, Marina).

Bottom's translation or metamorphosis was taken partly from Reginald Scot and partly from Apuleius, but the story has obvious links with the tale of Beauty and the Beast. As with the Ghost in *Hamlet* we can see that Shakespeare combined his knowledge of folklore with literary sources and imaginative inventions of his own.

Ironically enough, he makes Theseus say:

> I never may believe
> These antique fables, nor these fairy toys,

because, as he says, the lunatic, the lover and the poet 'are of imagination all compact.' Hippolyta protests that the various stories of the lovers support each other and 'More witnesseth than fancy's images.' Shakespeare's most fantastic play, in which we are asked to believe the impossible — and even the incompatible and, indeed, in which we do believe while we are in the theatre — is the best example of giving to airy nothing a local habitation and a name. But it is also a satirical comment on adolescent love, and it is linked to the world of the audience by the explanation provided of the atrocious summer of 1593 (or whenever it was).[4]

Let us turn finally to the question of witchcraft. In appearance the Weird Sisters seem to be traditional witches. Withered, wild in their attire, with chapped fingers, skinny lips and beards — the kind of old women who, because of their appearance, get credited by the villagers with possessing supernatural powers — and if a cow dies or a child falls sick they get the blame for it. The speech of Mother Sawyer in *The Witch of Edmonton* shows the results of such suspicions. (It was acted by Dame Edith Evans in a production by Michel St. Denis which I regard as the finest production of any Elizabethan or Jacobean play in my lifetime.) Mother Sawyer asks:

> And why on me? Why should the envious world

Throw all their scandalous malice upon me?
'Cause I am poor, deform'd and ignorant,
And like a bow buckled and bent together,
By some more strong in mischiefs than myself?
Must I for that be made a common sink
For all the filth and rubbish of men's tongues
To fall and run into? Some call me witch;
And being ignorant of myself, they go
About to teach me how to be one.

The Weird Sisters in *Macbeth* are given other characteristics of witches — their treasuring of fragments of dead bodies (a pilot's thumb, a finger of a birth-strangled babe); their revengefulness, exhibited in the harrying of the sailor whose wife had refused to give the witch some chestnuts; their control over winds; their seeing into the future; the limitation of their powers:

> his bark cannot be lost,
> Yet it shall be tempest-tossed;

All these would not surprise members of the original audience, and even the horrid ingredients of the cauldron would be acceptable as the kind of brew witches might be expected to make. Yet we should note that they are never called witches but only the Weird Sisters, and that Holinshed describes them in quite different terms as:

> resembling creatures of elder world...either the Weird Sisters, that is (as ye would say) the goddesses of destiny, or else some nymphs or feiries, indued with knowledge of prophecy by their necromantical science.

This made Kittredge identify the Weird Sisters as Norns, and he went on to say that:

> They are not hags in the service of the devil; they are not mere personifications of a man's evil desires or his ruthless craving for power. They are as actual and objective as the Furies that lie about the fugitive Orestes.

He adds; 'If they choose to wear the garb of witches for a time, that is their own affair.'

Whether we accept Kittredge's views or not, we should remember that Shakespeare was writing a play to be performed before James I, and that he had taken the precaution of reading some of his royal patron's works, including *Daemonology.* Echoes from that book occur several times in the course of the play. James comments, for example on the way devils foretell the future:

It is true that he knows not all things future, but yet that he knows part.

He says that witches might foretell 'what side shall win any battle, and that the devil makes 'himself to be trusted in these little things that he may have the better commodity thereafter to deceive them in the end with a trick once for all: I mean the everlasting perdition of their soul and body... He is able to deceive us to our wrack.' So Banquo warns Macbeth:

Oftentimes to win us to our harm
The instruments of darkness tell us truths,
Win us with honest trifles, to betray us
In deepest consequence.

The devil's agents:

creepe in credit with Princes by foretelling great things, part true, part false. For if all were false he would tune credit at all hands; but always doubtsome, as his oracles were.

James declares that witches are:

enticed either for the desire of revenge, or wordly riches, their whole practises are either to hurt men and their goods, or what they possess:... or else by the wrack in whatsoever sort of any whom God will permit them to have power of.

The Weird Sisters are not motivated in this way in their temptation of Macbeth, and it is one of the arguments against the authenticity of the Hecate scene — or at least against its being a part of the play as written in 1606 — that the Weird

Sisters become ordinary witches. In the play as originally written, Shakespeare sets going in our minds conflicting impressions of the Weird Sisters — sometimes witches, at other times devils in the shape of witches, tempting Macbeth in order to bring about his damnation, sometimes relying on popular conceptions of witchcraft, at other times echoing the learned King James and also influenced by classical stories of witchcraft in Ovid, in Lucan and in Apuleius. In this case, as with ghosts and fairies, Shakespeare underpinned and counter-pointed current superstitions with theological speculation and classical information.

It is possible, as H. M. Paul argued in his book on *Macbeth*, that Shakespeare's interest in Reginald Scot and Samuel Harsnet indicated that he did not share the credulities of most of his contemporaries, although it has been suggested that his interest in Harsnet's book was due to curiosity about the career of a former Stratford schoolmaster. But if one can judge from his writings, the two renaissance writers with whose temperaments he had most in common were Erasmus and Montaigne; but whereas they expressed their views in their own person, Shakespeare quite properly hides behind his *dramatis personae*. We do not know what he himself thought of ghosts, fairies and witches. All we do know is that he made dramatic use of them, as he did of dragon and phoenix, anthropophagi and centaurs, Caliban and Ariel, of the bed-trick so offensive to modern purists, of a statue which comes to life, of drugs which counterfeit death, and many other things for which he asks us to suspend our disbelief.

Elizabethan dramatists had to appeal on several different levels and, despite the difficulties involved, this prevented them from being coterie dramatists.

Some spectators of Act 4 of *The Winter's Tale* would recognize the sheep-shearing feast as an idealized version of what took place in their own villages, including nosegays for the shearers. There was still a kind of feast at Ilmington and Long Marston in the yearly years of this century. Other members of the audience would associate the feast with what they had read in *Daphnis and Chloe* or modern works in the tradition of Greek romances. The mention of Whitsun Pastorals would remind older members of the audience of entertainments they had seen in their youth and Perdita's mention of Proserpine, the spring goddess, would remind the educated of the various interpretations of the Proserpine story (which Leonard Digges discussed in the preface to his translation of Claudian's poem a year or two later) and the appropriateness of that story to the theme of *The Winter's Tale.* When Perdita returns to Sicilia, she is hailed by Leontes as 'Goddess', welcome as the spring to the earth. She is identified in the imagination of the audience with the goddess of whom she has spoken.

NOTES

1. F. Thistleton Dyer, *Folk Lore of Shakespeare* (London, 1883).
2. Batford: London, 1976.
3. When Falstaff exclaims 'Heaven defend me from that Welsh fairy', we are surely meant to think that he has recognized Parson Evans.
4. It may be mentioned that Drayton's overrated poem 'Nymphidia' follows Shakespeare in many of its details — especially in the minute size of the fairies. (This was not, I think, because both poets came from Warwickshire). The walls of Oberon's palace are made of spiders' legs, the Queen's bower is a cowslip, four nimble gnats draw her chariot and the wheels are made of crickets' bones. Mercutio, you will recall, makes Mab's whip of cricket's bone. Puck goes through brake and through briar, like the fairy in the *Dream*: and as the lovers in the play are prevented from fighting by an artificial darkness, so Oberon and Pigwiggen (what a name!) are prevented from fighting a duel by an artificial fog conjured up by Proserpine.

4
The Texts of *King Lear*:
An Interim Assessment of
the Controversy

The last of the New Arden editions of Shakespeare's plays appeared in 1982. A new General Editor, Richard Proudfoot was appointed, and the publishers decided to start again with a new 'New Arden'. Many of the original editors are dead — Ridley, Cairncross, Nosworthy, Lever, Ure, Maxwell, Leech — and for their ten plays other editors will have to be found. But I was urged to re-edit *Macbeth* and *King Lear,* two of the earliest volumes in the series (1951–2) and last revised in 1972. There will be no major changes in *Macbeth*, but *King Lear* is another matter. During the last thirty years there have been several important books written on the play, there have been some memorable performances, and I myself have written several articles on the play, setting forth my changing attitudes. But these facts are of minor importance compared with the textual revolution, of which the first rumblings were heard at the Washington Congress of the International Shakespeare Association in 1976.

Until 1975 it was taken for granted by all editors, whether wise or foolish, competent or incompetent, conservative or radical, that their duty was to conflate the original texts of 1608 and 1623, and, with one notable exception, they agreed to take the First Folio as their copy-text. Now a group of textual critics in England and the United States has claimed that such a conflated text is illegitimate, since it creates a play that was never performed in Shakespeare's lifetime, and that therefore an editor should print two separate texts, one based on the First Quarto and the other on the Folio. It is this new and proselytizing orthodoxy which it is my aim to question in the present article.

Let me begin by making four admissions: 1. Where it can be shown that lines in the Folio (F) text were meant to replace those in the Quarto (Q), we should not print both. The Quarto lines should be printed only in the notes. 2. When one has been familiar with the play for many years — I myself directed a performance half a century ago — it is impossible to banish from one's mind speeches which one has heard on the lips of Olivier or Gielgud, and hard to admit that Shakespeare deleted them. The textual Reformers (if I may so call them) may be justified in regarding such an attitude as reactionary prejudice. 3. Two separate texts of the play, threatened by both the Oxford and Cambridge editors, will inevitably cause a good deal of alarm and despondency among teachers, students, actors, and the general reader. But, of course, this ought not to weigh too heavily against the demands of scholarship. 4. Two more books on the controversy have been announced, so that this article can only be regarded as an interim assessment.

Meanwhile it can be said that the argument of the Reformers, indeed the *only* argument, is that the Folio text represents a radical revision by Shakespeare himself, and that his responsibility for the changes is proved by their brilliance. It is my contention that the argument rests on iterated assertions, that some of the alterations are dramatically disastrous, and that we ought (in Hamlet's words) to demand 'grounds more relative than this'.

The first shot in the campaign was fired by Michael J. Warren in April 1976. It was published, somewhat expanded, in the *Proceedings of the Conference*[1] as 'Quarto and Folio of *King Lear* and the Interpretation of Albany and Edgar'. Warren argues quite fairly that:

> it is not demonstrably erroneous to work with the possibility (a) that there may be no single 'ideal play' of *King Lear*, that there may never have been one, and that what we create by conflating both texts is merely an invention of editors and scholars; (b) that for all its problems Q is an authoritative version of the play; and (c) that F may indeed be a revised version of the play, that its

additions and omissions may constitute Shakespeare's considered modification of the earlier text, and we certainly cannot know that they are not.

Warren proceeds to show that the dialogue when Lear discovers Kent in the stocks differs in the two texts, and that the Folio's is intended as a replacement for the Quarto's and that therefore we ought not to print both.[2] Here I agree; but as the Quarto has clearly muddled the passage, I suspect that all the Folio has done is to *restore* what Shakespeare originally wrote.

Warren goes on to argue that the alterations in the last two acts of the play were carefully designed (by Shakespeare himself) to reduce the importance of Albany and increase the importance of Edgar. We may allow that this is the effect of the alterations, but it may be doubted whether they were so designed; and even if this was the purpose of the changes, they could be the result of a change in the cast. Most of the alterations are savage cuts, and cuts are usually motivated by the need to shorten a play, *King Lear* being one of the longest. Certainly Edgar takes from Albany the last speech of the play, either as the future king or because the words 'we that are young' are more appropriate to him. Warren, I think, indulges in a good deal of special pleading, as when he asserts that:

> The absence of Edgar's moral meditation from the end of III.vi brings the speech at IV.iv.1 into sharp focus, isolating it more obviously between the blinding and entrance of Gloucester: in F the two servants do not remain on stage after Cornwall's exit. The additional lines at this point emphasize the hollowness of Edgar's assertions; while the quantity of sententiousness is reduced, its nature is made more emphatically evident. Edgar gains in prominence, ironically enough, by the loss of a speech, and the audience becomes more sharply aware of his character.

This last sentence is difficult to swallow: and the whole paragraph seems to me to be evasive. Of course Edgar's moralizing is frequently upset by the realities he has to face, as Albany's is too. But Warren slides over the dialogue between Cornwall's servants after the blinding scene (which is discussed below), and he is not aware of the positive merits of Edgar's rhymed soliloquy at the end of Act 3 Scene 6. He reminds one of theatre directors who call for the scissors as soon as they see a passage in rhyme. During the whole of the act Edgar has been posing as Poor Tom, and he has been given only one brief aside in his own person. The soliloquy is therefore important to him as a character. He plays so many parts in the course of the play that we are liable to lose sight of the man behind the masks. The lines, moreover, make two vital dramatic points. They make the first verbal link between the two plots — 'He childed as I fathered' — and they emphasize that the mental suffering of the king is harder to bear than the physical suffering of the Bedlam beggar, though he too has had more than his share of mental suffering in being rejected by the father he loves:

> When we our betters see bearing our woes,
> We scarcely think our miseries our foes...
> How light and portable my pain seems now,
> When that which makes me bend makes the King bow.
>   (III.vi.102-4, 108-9)

Now if Shakespeare was indeed responsible for this cut, he was presumably also responsible for the addition of the Fool's prophecy at the end of Act 3 Scene 2. Neither the addition nor the subtraction would seem to be the work of a supreme dramatist.

Warren mentions that the cuts in Act 4 Scene 2 severely reduce Albany's theatrical impact, so that he appears more futile, 'less obviously a man capable of action'. His most powerful speech (IV.ii.46ff.) is dismissed as 'a pious pronouncement'. But this, and his later speech on hearing of Cornwall's death ('This shows you are above, you justicers'), although they may exhibit Albany's illusions about a divinely ordered universe, are very necessary to the poetic framework of the play, with its varied and conflicting attitudes to the gods.[3] In any case, Warren gives not a single dramatic, or even theatrical, reason for spoiling Albany's part. Perhaps the company found that the actor just was not adequate for the part.

Steven Urkowitz devotes a chapter to the alterations in Albany's character, caused particularly by the omissions in Act 4 Scene 2.[4] He points out that:

The lines omitted from F are precisely those stressing Albany's conscious articulation of, and personal adherence to, the value of respect for parents and benefactors. The lines remaining... are those expressing his new hostility to his wife, but they yield no hint of his own beliefs... The references to 'origin', 'sap' and 'branch' assert Albany's association with a positive, natural value system. They are not in the Folio.

Urkowitz goes on to point out that Albany's 'references to wisdom, goodness, grace, reverence and the obligation to gratitude are removed' so that only two speeches declare his moral system. In the Folio, Urkowitz claims, Albany 'seems to espouse no positively defined ethical standards'. This, he concludes, was the purpose of the alterations.

To this one must object that there seems to be no dramatic point in the alterations, and that the defence of the cuts is so feeble that it can hardly increase our confidence that they were Shakespeare's own. As two moral speeches are retained, it is absurd to pretend that Albany is deprived of defined ethical standards. Moreover, in the last scene of the play, Albany plainly expresses those standards. Presumably the cuts in Act 4 Scene 2 were made because the play was thought to be too long — possibly for a provincial tour — and they castrated Albany's part: it is surely probable that the mangling was not deliberate, but an unfortunate and inadvertent result of the cuts.

Gary Taylor, while making legitimate points about the treatment of the war in Quarto and the Folio, goes out of his way to approve both of the cuts in Albany's part and of the dialogue between Cornwall's servants:[5]

We surely no longer need to be told, by Edgar, or the two servants or Albany or Cordelia, what to think of the two sisters' treatment of Lear and Gloucester. Albany need not go on at such length in IV.ii in order to motivate his eventual repudiation of his wife in V.iii; so horrendous are the events of Acts 2 and 3 that we will easily infer that Albany's feelings are similar to our own.

Apart from the fact that this conflicts with Urkowitz's views, it is surely a peculiar line of argument, a strange notion of drama. The point of Albany's speeches is not to motivate his

later repudiation of Goneril — obviously he repudiates her in
Act 4 Scene 2. The various comments by the good characters
on the deeds of the evil ones are felt by the audience to be a
necessary expression of our sense of outrage. The multiple
choric effects of the speeches of sympathetic characters are an
essential part of Shakespeare's method. To cut them out will
leave us feeling deprived, if not in a moral vacuum. Some
modern directors, indeed, have gone as far as they dare to make
us irritated with Albany and Edgar, if not yet with Cordelia,
and to sympathize with Edmund and Goneril.

Steven Urkowitz is another critic who approves of the
cutting of the dialogue between Cornwall's servants. He
points out that the servants' plan 'is at odds with how the
meeting between Gloucester and Edgar occurs in the next
scene'. Moreover, and more importantly, 'the statement of the
plan removes the theatrical element of surprise, that is clearly
intended in the design of Act 4 Scene 1. The meeting, Urkowitz
thinks, 'should be a surprise to the Old Man who is leading
Gloucester, to Gloucester himself, to Edgar, and especially to
the audience'. He argues that Gloucester's 'accidental meeting
with Edgar', his plan to use Poor Tom as a guide, despite the
Old Man's objections, are the things which cause the poignancy of the scene. To which one may retort that the upsetting
of the servants' plan is itself a surprise, that Shakespeare often,
even usually, writes scenes which happen differently from what
he had led us to expect, that the real poignancy of the scene
depends on the meeting of the son with the father who cannot
see him, and that there are two cogent reasons why the cutting
of the servants' dialogue is a dramatic disaster. Philip Edwards
has eloquently expressed one of the reasons:[6]

> The moment of stillness provided by the shock and compassion of
> the servants in Q is a theatrical experience of the highest order.
> Whoever cut the scene failed to grasp its theatrical imaginative-
> ness as well as its thematic importance, and he could hardly have
> been Shakespeare.

The second reason I put forward with some satisfaction, as
Urkowitz has branded me as an academic with no practical

knowledge of the stage. In the production of the play I
directed in the thirties in collaboration with a professional
actress and also in the Leeds production in 1951 when Wilson
Knight played Lear and I was Gloucester, we found on both
occasions that after the blinding, and despite an interval
between Acts 3 and 4, Gloucester had very little time between
his exit in Act 3 Scene 7 and his reappearance in Act 4 Scene 1
to change his clothes or put on a cloak and to have his eyes
bandaged. Even with the additional two-and-a-half lines in
Edgar's opening soliloquy, Gloucester has only fourteen lines
in the wings if we stick to the Folio text. It is not enough.[7]
Apart from its dramatic value, the dialogue between the
servants is a theatrical necessity. Either the cut was made
accidentally by the Folio compositor, or the cut was not
Shakespeare's.[8] Anyone who saw the Peter Brook production
of the play will remember the dire effect of the omission of this
scene; and this was the director's aim. He wanted to eliminate
this trace of humanity, so that he could enrol Shakespeare as a
forerunner of the Theatre of Cruelty.

Another cut in the Folio is the mock trial of Goneril and
Regan in Act 3 Scene 6. Gary Taylor argues that the purpose of
this cut was to stream-line the plot. One has only to look at the
second act of *Hamlet* to know that streamlining was not
always one of Shakespeare's priorities — perhaps it never was.
Streamlining is the tragic flaw of certain directors who imagine
that a play is more dramatic if it is stripped of its poetry.[9]
Perhaps the real reason for the omission of the mock trial was
that it was unsuccessful in performance, the original audience
not having read Wilson Knight on the grotesque element in
the play. Even today it is the hardest scene to stage; yet, as
Ronald Peacock has finely said: 'It is an illumination that
produces from the subconscious the effect of order'.[10]

To consider all the passages discussed by the Reformers in
their attempt to prove that the Folio represents an inspired
revision by Shakespeare himself would require a fair-sized
volume. All I can hope to do in this article is to take seven or
eight typical passages — and they are genuinely typical. The
first I have chosen is the dialogue between Edmund and Edgar
at the end of Act 1 Scene 2. Instead of a cut, it consists of a
substantial addition to the Quarto text:

(Q)	*Bast.*	That's my feare brother, I aduise you to the best, goe arm'd.
(F)	*Edm.*	That's my feare, I pray you haue a continent forbearance till the speed of his rage goes slower: and as I say, retire with me to my lodging, from whence I will fitly bring you to heare my Lord speake: pray ye goe, there's my key: if you do stirre abroad, goe arm'd.
	Edg.	Arm'd, Brother?
	Edm.	Brother, I aduise you to the best.

The Folio version is manifestly a great improvement. It makes Edmund's deception of his brother more plausible. Where I differ from the Reformers is that I do not believe this was part of the revision. It is much more likely that the Quarto compositor (or whoever compiled the text) eye-skipped from 'That's my fear, brother' to 'brother', accidentally omitting the intervening passage. The Quarto passage, feeble as it is, can hardly be what Shakespeare ever wrote. The original was happily restored in the Folio apart from the omission of 'brother' after 'feare'.

The next passage (I.iv.310 ff.) is also an addition in the Folio text, and it too is an obvious improvement.

(Q)	*Gon.*	Doe you marke that my Lord?
	Duke.	I cannot bee so partiall *Gonorill* to the great loue I beare you.
	God.	Come sir no more, you, more knaue then foole, after your master?
	Foole.	Nunckle *Lear*...(*three lines omitted*)
	Gon.	What *Oswald*, ho. *Oswald.* Heere Madam.
	Gon.	What haue you writ this letter to my sister?

(F)	*Gon.*	Do you marke that?
	Alb.	I cannot be so partiall, *Gonerill*. To the great loue I beare you.
	Gon.	Pray you content. What *Oswald*, hoa? You sir, more Knaue then Foole, after your Master.
	Foole.	Nunkle *Lear*, Nunkle *Lear*... (*6 lines omitted*)
	Gon.	This man hath had good counsell, A hundred Knights?

              'Tis politike, and safe to let him keepe
              At point a hundred Knights: yes, that on euerie
                 dreame,
              Each buz, each fancie, each complaint, dislike,
              He may enguard his dotage with their powres,
              And hold our liues in mercy. *Oswald*, I say.
Alb.   Well, you may feare too farre.
Gon.   Safer than trust too farre;
              Let me still take away the harmes I feare,
              Not feare still to be taken. I know his heart,
              What he hath vtter'd I haue writ my Sister:
              If she sustaine him, and his hundred Knights
              When I haue shew'd th'vnfitnesse.
                  Enter Steward
              How now *Oswald*?
              What haue you writ that Letter to my Sister?

The extra lines spoken by Goneril are a valuable addition to the text. As Urkowitz says, 'by introducing a delay between the time she calls for Oswald and the time he appears' she is shown to be 'thinking aloud during the intervals between her brusque commands'. What is more important, perhaps, is that her complaint about Lear's knights and her fear that they will prove dangerous is a useful preparation for her later conduct and goes some way to excuse Albany's tame acquiescence. This may be a rewriting of the Quarto version, as the Reformers assume. But as the basis and nature of the Quarto are still a matter of controversy — which may be settled when Peter Blayney's second volume appears — it may well be that the Folio text represents not a revision but a restoration.

    The next problem is afforded by adjacent passages in Act 3 Scene 1, one in the Quarto only, the other in the Folio only.

(Q)   *Albany* and *Cornwall*
           But true it is, from *France*, there comes a power
           Into this scattered kingdome, who alreadie wise in our
              negligence
           Haue secret feet in some of our best Ports,
           And are at point to shew their open banner,
           Now to you, if on my credit you dare build so farre
           To make your speed to Douer, you shall find
           Some that will thanke you, making iust report

Of how vnnatural and bemadding sorrow
The King hath cause to plaine.
I am a Gentleman of blood and breeding,
And from some knowledge and assurance
Offer this office to you.

(F)   Albany, and Cornwall:
Who haue, as who haue not, that their great Starres
Thron'd and set high: Seruants, who seeme no lesse,
Which are to France the Spies and Speculations
Intelligent of our State. What hath bin seene,
Either in snuffes, and packings of the Dukes,
Or the hard Reine, which both of them hath borne
Against the old kinde King; or something deeper,
Whereof (perchance) these are but furnishings.

The Reformers think that the lines in the Folio were meant to replace those in the Quarto. To me both texts seem inadequate as they stand. I suspect that the Folio lines were written on a slip of paper attached to the Quarto text (as was the custom) and that the Folio compositor wrongly supposed that the passage was meant to replace the Quarto lines. It is true that the retention of both passages involves an awkward join, and this may be due to the loss of one or more lines.[11]

The next alteration to be discussed is the total omission in the Folio of a whole scene (Act 4 Scene 3) in which there is some discussion of the King of France's departure, followed by an account of the reception by Cordelia of the news of her father's treatment, and the information that Lear is in Dover, and that, because of his feelings of shame, Lear refuses to see Cordelia. Urkowitz complains that this scene conflicts with what we learn later — that Lear does not mention Cordelia's presence in Britain, that in neither Act 4 Scene 6 nor Act 4 Scene 7 does he express shame, that he is surprised to see Cordelia when he awakens, thinking her a spirit, and that in Act 4 scene 4 he is in the country, not in the town. Taylor adds two other points: that to give a reason for the French King's absence 'raises an awkward question, which would be better left unasked' — the Folio has Cordelia, not Le Far in command, thus camouflaging that it is a foreign invasion — and that it is more immediately satisfying to see and hear Cordelia than to be told about her.[12] I agree with Taylor's first point, that the explanation of the French King's return is feeble; but he does not appreciate the serious disadvantage of omitting the account of Cordelia in this scene. She has been absent from the stage for 2,000 lines — the length of some of Shakespeare's entire plays — and she will have a difficult entrance in the next scene unless the audience has been reminded of her. She is presumably dressed as a soldier and some who have not read the play will wonder 'Who is she?' or even 'Who is he?' Cordelia's part, moreover is the tiniest of any major Shakespearean character — just over 100 lines, and she often speaks in monosyllables. The account of her weeping and Kent's comment on this help to build up her importance in the scheme of the play.

Urkowitz's complaints seem to me to be frivolous. It is made clear that it is only in his lucid moments (his 'better time') that Lear remembers the situation, that his escape to the country in Act 4 Scene 4 is not inconsistent with the account in Act 4 Scene 3, that he is described as 'mad as the vexed sea', that he is clearly mad through Act 4 Scene 6, and that he recovers his senses in Act 4 Scene 7. His kneeling to Cordelia is the expression of his sovereign shame. Urkowitz seems to expect a madman to behave rationally and consistently. It is surely obvious that the motive of the cut is not to improve the play by subtle alterations, but simply to reduce its length.

Urkowitz also congratulates Shakespeare for cutting the last twelve lines of Act 4 Scene 7, after the exit of Lear and Cordelia, on the grounds that only in the Folio version 'does the audience see . . . contrasting images following one another' i.e. the moving scene of the reunion of Lear and Cordelia, followed immediately by the entrance of Edmund and Regan. This comment is not merely insensitive, it is lacking in theatrical understanding. The audience needs a moment to wipe away their tears; they also need to be told that Edmund is leading Regan's forces, and they can appreciate the way of the rumour that Edgar is with Kent in Germany and Kent's dry comment, 'Report is changeable':

> *Gent.*   Holds it true sir that the Duke of *Cornwall* was so
>   slaine?

Kent   Most certaine sir.
Gent. Who is conductor of his people?
Kent   As tis said, the bastard sonne of *Gloster*.
Gent. They say *Edgar* his banisht sonne is with the Earl of
         Kent in *Germanie*.
Kent   Report is changeable, tis time to looke about,
         The powers of the kingdome approach apace.
Gent. The arbiterment is like to be bloudie, fare you well, sir.
Kent   My poynt and period will be throughly wrought,
         Or well, or ill, as this dayes battels fought.   *Exit.*

An even more blatant example of special pleading is
Urkowitz's comment on the omission by the Folio of the lines
given to the Captain who agrees to murder Lear and Cordelia:

I cannot draw a cart nor eat dried oats.
If it be man's work, I'll do't.

Urkowitz remarks that:

Instead of seeing the Captain explain his moral subjugation to the
force of corrupt power, the audience watches Edmund drive him
to his task, and then immediately turns to see Albany, Goneril and
Regan enter. In the Folio the Bastard is the only active figure and
the important focus of attention. His agent is practically mute —
a figure, not a character. Although the Q text gives us a Captain
vividly realized in only a dozen or so words [Here Urkowitz
reveals his sovereign shame at his own argument] the line seems to
have been cut in order to allow Edmund to be shown at his most
villainous moment, against a neutral rather than against a lively
background.

My disagreement here is not that Urkowitz is substituting a
theatrical for a dramatic or poetic effect, but that he seems to
be ignorant of the way audiences behave. They would never
want to sacrifice such a condensed biography and such a
revelation of character. The cut is too silly even for those who
perpetrated the others: it must have been accidental.

My last example of inauspicious cuts is the account given by
Edgar of his meeting with the dying Kent:

Edg.   This would haue seemd a periode to such

As loue not sorrow, but another to amplifie too much
Would make much more, and top extremitie,
Whil'st I was big in clamor, came there in a man,
Who hauing seene me in my worst estate,
Shund my abhord society, but then finding
Who twas that so indur'd with his strong armes
He fastened on my necke and bellowed out,
As hee'd burst heauen, threw me [him] on my father,
Told the most pitious tale of *Lear* and him
 That euer eare receiued, which in recounting
His griefe grew puissant and the strings of life,
Began to cracke [,] twice then the trumpets sounded.
And there I left him traunst.

Alb.   But who was this?

Edg.   *Kent,* sir, the banisht *Kent,* who in disguise,
Followed his enemie king and did him seruice
Improper for a slaue.

Gary Taylor thinks that the lines were omitted 'to reinforce an audience's interest in the long gap between Lear's exit with Cordelia and his entrance with her body'. Warren, on the other hand, thinks that Edgar in the Quarto version was too much concerned for his own dramatic role and that this cut (among others) reduces somewhat 'his callowness, his easy indulgence of his sensibility in viewing the events through which he is living'. Apart from this questionable assessment of Edgar's character, both comments are beside the point. It shortens the gap between Lear's two appearances by only a minute; and the suspense between Edmund's order for the murder and his decision to reveal it is a vital factor in the last scene of the play. Above all, Edgar's account is a necessary introduction to Kent't appearance eight lines later. His role in the last minutes of the play would otherwise be obscure to those who had not perused Bradley's *Shakespearean Tragedy.*

It will be gathered from my comments on particular passages that I do not believe that the Folio alterations were made by Shakespeare himself in order to improve the play. I cannot agree with Ernst Honigmann that only Shakespeare 'was capable of thinking at this level'.[13] Some of the additions — perhaps, as I believe, all of them — restore the Quarto's accidental omissions. There are a very few genuine substitutions which may likewise restore what Shakespeare originally wrote. But the savage cuts in the second half of the play had the sole purpose of reducing its length. It is a long play, and Shakespeare may have been reluctantly responsible for cutting it down to size, but the cuts may have been made when he was no longer there to protest. A few of the changes were probably designed to make a foreign invasion less offensive to an English audience, but the alterations in the characters of Edgar and Albany were a fortuitous result of the cuts, not the purpose of them.

Some of the changes seem to have been made because of a reduced cast — perhaps for a tour.[14] At IV.vi.186 three gentlemen enter in pursuit of Lear, according to the Quarto; in the Folio there is only one.

Given other circumstances, some or all the cuts might have been restored. It is clear that a modern director has every excuse to ignore the cuts. It may also follow, that despite the deplorable state of the text, the Quarto would better serve as the basis for a modern edition than the Folio. An editor would be foolish to omit, or to relegate to the notes, the passages so savagely pruned in 1623. The cuts do not improve the play: they damage it fatally. Whoever was responsible was the first of the vandals, to be followed by Tate and a long line of actor-managers and directors.

POSTSCRIPT

The Division of the Kingdoms, edited by Gary Taylor and Michael Warren, appeared in 1983 after this article was in the press. The contributors to this symposium are less anxious to argue that the Folio changes are all improvements, but there is still some special pleading. They give good grounds for believing that Shakespeare made a large number of small changes at the time when the cuts were made. Taylor, the author of the longest chapter, makes use of Eliot Slater's vocabulary tests to suggest that the revisions were made at the same date as *Cymbeline*, possibly for the opening of Blackfriars. I have some doubts about the validity of the tests, by which Slater purported to prove that Shakespeare wrote the whole of *Edward III*, which I find difficult to believe. Moreover, the words peculiar to the Folio make too small a sample on which to base definite conclusions. Nevertheless, I am prepared to accept Taylor's date for the revisions, and that they were not simply restorations of a text mangled by the Quarto compositors. Only Stone, as far as I know, imagined that Massinger was responsible for the alterations, so that this section of Taylor's chapter was hardly necessary.

I remain convinced that the cuts — as opposed to the minor changes — were deplorable; and that the modification of the characters of Albany, Kent and Edgar were the result of the cuts, not the motive for them. Shakespeare may have made the cuts himself, however reluctantly, or he may have found that they had been made by others to shorten the play, or for theatrical reasons of a temporary nature. We should not pretend that the results are a matter for congratulation. Gary Taylor believes that he is a spokesman for theatrical intelligence. He supposes that our objections to the cut at the end of Act 3 are those of 'literary' critics, incapable of seeing the dramatic advantage of omitting 'explicit moral commentary'. This leaves me speechless. Explicit moral commentary has been a feature of all great drama from Aeschylus to the present day. I may add that my experience of the play in the theatre extends over 55 years, and it includes directing the play at York and playing the part of Gloucester at Leeds, both before Gary Taylor was born. I may be wrong; but if I am, it is not because I have a literary rather than a properly theatrical attitude to the play.

NOTES

1. Michael J. Warren, 'Quarto and Folio of *King Lear* and the Interpretation of Albany and Edgar' in *Pattern of Excelling Nature*, ed David Bevington and Jay L. Halio (Delaware University Press: Newark, 1978).
2. *King Lear,* II.iv.12-23.
3. William R. Elton, *King Lear and the Gods* (Huntington Library San Marino, 1966), *passim*.

4.   Steven Urkowitz, *Shakespeare's Revision of 'King Lear'* (Princeton, 1980).
5.   Gary Taylor, 'The War in *King Lear*', Shakespeare Survey 33 (1980), pp. 27-34.
6.   Philip Edwards' review of Urkowitz's book, *Modern Language Review*, July 1982.
7.   The reformers are driven to suggest that there were intervals after each act.
8.   I am reminded of a small cut in *Cymbeline* made by a director at Stratford. He found at the dress rehearsal that Imogen did not have time to change into her night-gown.
9.   If one examines the prompt-book of *The Elder Statesman* one finds that T. S. Eliot was apparently allowed to retain only one image in the last scene, the characteristic 'As the asthmatic struggles for breath'.
10. Ronald Peacock, *The Poet in the Theatre* (Routledge: London, 1946).
11. Or Kent may break off in the middle of a sentence. Urkowitz wittily retorts that the transition between the two sections of Kent's speech 'is more a bibliographical quirk than a dramatic subtlety'.
12. Taylor, *op. cit.*
13. The Library, June 1982, p. 155.
14. Greg pointed out (*Review of English Studies*, 1940, p. 302) that no alcove and probably no balcony would be needed; and this suggests that the cut version may have been made for touring purposes.

5

Theophanies in the Last Plays

Everyone notices that, whereas no gods or goddesses appear in any of Shakespeare's plays written before 1607, there is hardly a play written after that date in which the gods do not intervene. This can partly be accounted for by the fact that nearly all the early plays are set in the Christian era. Hymen appears in *As You Like It,* but he is presumably played by one of the cast. In *King Lear,* when Albany prays for the safety of the king and Cordelia, he gets a notoriously dusty answer. Macduff wonders, after the murder of his family, at the non-intervention of the Heavens, but comes to the conclusion that his family were punished for his sins. In *King Lear,* as Willian Elton has urged, *deus* remains *absconditus*.[1] In *Coriolanus* the hero rhetorically pretends that the gods laugh at his surrender to Volumnia's pleading, though the general tone of the play is entirely secular. In *Antony and Cleopatra,* however, there are intimations of immortality, and it could almost be said that the protagonists are manifestations of pagan gods. It is not accidental that Cleopatra should be identified with Isis; that the meeting of the lovers on the river Cydmus should lead in Plutarch to a rumour that Venus and Bacchus had met 'for the general good of all Asia' and that Enobarbus should describe the meeting in hyperbolic terms with Cleopatra 'o'erpicturing' Venus; that Antony should refer to his ancestor, Hercules; that there should be supernatural music when the god deserts him; and that after his death Cleopatra should depict him as a demigod. But we are left at the end with the feeling that the lovers, who have been playing such exalted roles, may after all have been self-deluded and self-deceiving.

When we turn to *Pericles* there is a very great difference. We no longer see human beings aspiring to be demigods: we see the gods sporting with powerless human beings. Behind the actions

of the characters, and despite the textual uncertainties, we can
see the controlling power of Diana. Thaisa, before her hasty
marriage to Pericles, has vowed, according to her father, to
wear Diana's livery for a year:

> This by the eye of Cynthia hath she vow'd
> And on her virgin honour will not break it.
> *(Pericles*, II.v.11-12)

Diana, it would seem, punishes her for taking her name in
vain by making her die in childbirth, despite Pericles' prayer to
his 'divinest patroness,' Lucina, one of Diana's names. Thaisa's
first words when she is brought back to life are:

> O dear Diana, where am I?
> (Pericles, III.ii.110)

She decides to adopt the vestal livery she had formerly
promised to wear, and she wears it for some sixteen years as a
priestess in Diana's temple at Ephesus. Marina in the brothel
appropriately prays to the same goddess to protect her vir-
ginity (IV.ii.149). After Pericles has recovered his daughter
and heard (as he thinks) the music of the spheres, Diana
appears to him and commands him to visit her temple, so that
in the end he is reunited to Thaisa too. He might exclaim in
the words of the Bible, 'Great is Diana of the Ephesians!' It
should be added that neither Gower nor Twine refers to
Diana, except in connection with the temple where Thaisa
serves the goddess. In the good physician, Cerimon, we see 'a
heavenly effect in an earthly actor'; or, as Thaisa puts it: 'this
man/Through whom the gods have shown their power':
(V.iii.61).

Apart from Diana, the god who most affects the fortunes of
Pericles, though he does not make a personal appearance, is
Neptune. Pericles is wrecked on the shore at Pentapolis, where
he meets Thaisa. On the voyage from Pentapolis there is a
storm, during which Marina is born and Thaisa is cast over-
board, apparently dead. Thereafter, we are told, Pericles gives
himself up 'to the mask'd Neptune'. After the report of
Marina's death, he arrives at Mytilene, his ship adorned with

sable banners, while the city is celebrating the feast of Neptune. It cannot be accidental that this is the beginning of the end of his trials and tribulations.

The misfortunes of Pericles, at least in the play as we have it, seem too arbitrary, and it is possible, as I have suggested elsewhere,[2] that Shakespeare made more than either the reporter or the compositor did of the broken vow to Diana, her punishment and ultimate forgiveness of Thaisa. But the new dimension apparent in *Pericles* can be seen by comparing it with one of Shakespeare's earliest plays, *The Comedy of Errors*. In its source, the father of the twins had died long before: Shakespeare begins his play with Ægeon, condemned to death in the opening scene, and reprieved in the last. Memories of the story of Apollonius of Tyre lie at the back of the denouement. The scene is set, like the final scene of *Pericles*, at Ephesus. The lost wife has become, not a priestess in the temple of Diana, but an abbess in an anachronistic priory; and she is reunited to her husband, like Thaisa, after a lapse of many years. Yet Shakespeare is vague about her religion, and there is no suggestion that the reunion of husband and wife is due to the workings of providence. God — and the gods — are excluded from the play, except for a reference by Ægeon in the first scene to their mercilessness.

In *Cymbeline*, which probably followed soon after *Pericles* Shakespeare avoided the mistake of having a nearly guiltless hero as the plaything of the immortals — a tennis-ball was the favourite Renaissance analogy — by making Posthumus Leonatus doubly guilty, of betting on his wife's chastity and of ordering her murder. The play, as has too often been demonstrated, is close in certain respects to *Philaster*; but neither in *Philaster*, nor in the Boccaccio story which provided Shakespeare with his main source, nor in *Frederyke of Jennen*, nor in the historical material taken from Holinshed, could he have found the vision of Jupiter in the last act. J. M. Nosworthy has convincingly shown[3] that Shakespeare remembered an old play, *The Rare Triumphs of Love and Fortune*, which opens with a quarrel between the gods and their attempted pacification by Jupiter:

Ye Gods and Goddesses, whence springes this strife of late?

Who are the authors of this mutenye?
Or whence hath sprung this civil discorde here:
Which on the sodaine strooke vs in this feare.
If Gods that raigne in Skyes doo fall at warre,
No meruaile then though mortall men doo iarre
. . . .
Ye powers deuine be reconciled againe,
Depart from discorde and extreme debate:
Within your breasts let loue and peace remaine,
A perfect patterne of your heauenly state.

(1-6.64-7)

In the last act of the play, Jupiter intervenes; the lovers
Hermione and Fidelia, are reconciled with the King, who had
previously banished Hermione as Posthumus had been banished in *Cymbeline*, and the King is reconciled with Hermione's father, the exiled Bomelio.

The vision vouchsafed to the sleeping Posthumus has not
found many admirers.[4] The ghosts squeak and gibber in the
metre that Chapman used when he spoke out loud and bold in
his translation of the *Iliad*; and though Jupiter is given the
dignity of rhymed pentameters, both they and the ghosts'
fourteeners seem wooden, coming as they do after the colloquial ease of Shakespeare's later blank verse. Still, when all is
said, there is no reason to drag in a hypothetical collaborator
to bear the responsibility of the passages we happen to dislike.
When one considers the other plays of Shakespeare's final
period, one is not surprised to find Jupiter making a personal
appearance in *Cymbeline*. Shakespeare knew that in such a
scene the spectacle and the music were more important than
the words, and he realized that the descent of Jove on the eagle
would keep the audience interested. What he was writing was
hardly more than a libretto, and we may suppose that both the
ghosts and Jupiter would adopt a special manner of delivery,
perhaps to a musical accompaniment.

The message conveyed by Jupiter is essentially the same as
that given in *The Rare Triumphs of Love and Fortune*:

But when the Sunne after a shower of raine,
Breakes through the Clowdes, and shows his might againe,
More comfortable [is] his glory then

Because it was a while withheld of men.
Peace after warre is pleasanter we finde,
A ioy differd is sweeter to the minde.

(1467-1472)

So Jupiter tells the ghosts:

Whom best I love I cross; to make my gift,
The more delay'd, delighted. Be content
....
He shall be lord of Lady Imogen,
And happier much by his affliction made.

(V.iv.92-108)

'The Lord Loveth whom he chasteneth', we are assured. Whether Posthumus will really be happier in his marriage when he and Imogen both know he had tried to have her murdered is a question which should not be asked in the world of the play. But at least Posthumus forgives Imogen and admists she is his superior, even when he still believes her guilty of adultery; he forgives freely the man who has tricked him into this belief; and Imogen forgives both the men who have wronged her.

This process of forgiveness, which is the main theme of the play, had been set in train before Jupiter's appearance which, it would seem, has no real influence on what happens: it merely informs the audience that all will come right in the end. Nevertheless, one gets the impression that the gods have been watching over their mortal favourite, and that what ultimately happens is in accordance with the divine will.

There is no actual theophany in *The Winter's Tale*, but we have a greater sense than in *Cymbeline* that human lives are watched over by the gods. This is due partly to what appears to be a direct intervention when Leontes denies the oracle and is immediately informed of the death of Mamillius. But it is also due to the way in which the riddling oracle holds out a promise that Perdita will be restored, and to the providential shipwreck on the coast of Bohemia so that Perdita, when she grows up, can reconcile Polixenes and Leontes by marrying Florizel.

There are other factors which have to be borne in mind. The Christian undertones of a pagan play have often been pointed out — the references to Judas, to original sin, to the need for repentance, to purgatory and redemption. Then there is Antigonus' vision of Hermione, which is comparable in some ways to the vision of Diana in *Pericles*. There is also, as critics have pointed out, a curious suggestion that underneath the conscious level of the play is a vegetation myth. Leonard Digges, Shakespeare's neighbour, published his translation of *The Rape of Proserpine* in 1617, not long after the first performances of *The Winter's Tale*, and his account of the significance of the poem contained nothing that was unfamiliar to the educated Jacobean reader. Apart from the allegorical significance, Digges points out that Ceres stands for tillage, Proserpine for the seeds, and Pluto for the earth. It is difficult to believe that some of Shakespeare's original audience would not have noticed his references to the story of Proserpine. Perdita plays as she has seen others do in Whitsun pastorals; she is called Flora by Florizel, and the sheepshearing:

> Is as a meeting of the petty gods,
> And you the Queen on't.
>
> (IV.iv.4-5)

She confesses that as the mistress of the feast she is 'most goddess-like prank'd up'. When she is distributing the summer flowers, she wishes she had spring flowers to distribute to her fellow-maidens, and she refers directly to the Proserpine story:

> O Proserpina,
> For the flowers now that, frighted, thou let'st fall
> From Dis's waggon! — daffodils
> That come before the swallow dares, and take
> The winds of March with beauty...
>
> (IV.iv.116-120)

When she arrives in Sicilia, Leontes immediately greets her as 'goddess', and that he is thinking of the spring goddess can be seen from his next speech:

> Welcome hither,
> As is the spring to th' earth.
>
> (V.i.151-2)

It is hardly too fanciful to suggest that the theophany in *The Winter's Tale* is the appearance of Perdita, and that the 'death' and 'resurrection' of Hermione provide a parallel to the period spent by Proserpine in the underworld and her return to earth.

There is no actual theophany in *The Tempest*, but Juno and Ceres are among the characters in the masque performed by the spirits. Prospero is the controller of the spirits and the deviser of the masque, as he is also the controller of the inhabitants and visitors of his island. It may be said, indeed, that the visitors are compelled to come and that they enact their own roles, but in a plot devised by Prospero so that, in relation to them, Prospero is omnipotent and omniscient, and to the audience he seems to shadow forth divine qualities because he wills himself to be controlled by 'god-like reason'. To perceptive members of the audience, therefore, there need not be any other manifestation of the divine. In *Cymbeline* Jupiter promises that all shall be well: and Imogen and Post-humus make it well by their acts of forgiveness. In *The Tempest* the rarer action of Prospero does not require a heavenly validation.

The vision of paradise granted to Queen Katherine in *Henry VIII* is another example of the masque elements in the plays of the period; but much more interesting from our point of view is *The Two Noble Kinsmen*. There is a kind of antemasque in Act 3 (for which Fletcher or Beaumont was doubtless responsible), and the scene in Act 5, in which the kinsmen and Emilia offer prayers to Mars, Venus and Diana, and all receive apparently favourably answers, is an impressive example of theophany. There is virtual unanimity that the scene was Shakespeare's own, and that even the stage direc-tions bear marks of his hand. Arcite's prayer to Mars contains some of Shakespeare's characteristic imagery and vocabulary:

> Thou mighty one, that with thy power hast turn'd
> Green Neptune into purple...
> > who dost pluck
> With hand armipotent from forth blue clouds
> The mason'd turrets, that both mak'st and break'st
> The stony girths of cities...
> > that heal'st with blood

> The earth when it is sick, and cur'st the world
> O'th'pleurisy of people.
>
> (V.i.49-66)

The other speeches are equally Shakespearian, although Palamon's to Venus reveals an extravagant satirical power unlike anything he had written before, even the satirical scenes of *Troilus and Cressida.* The gods do not make an appearance on the stage — their statues are an adequate substitute for that — but they manifest themselves by the signs they give their worshippers:

> there is heard clanging of armour,
> with a short thunder, as the
> burst of a battle...
>
> Here music is heard and doves are
> seen to flutter...
>
> Here the hind vanishes under the
> altar and in the place ascends
> a rose-tree, having one rose upon it
> . . . .
> Here is heard a sudden twang of
> instruments and the rose falls from
> the tree.
>
> (V.i.61-136)

Arcite takes Mars's signs auspiciously, Palamon gives Venus thanks for 'this fair token', and Emilia declares that Diana's 'signs were gracious'. As it turns out, the prayers are all answered literally: Arcite wins the fight but loses the lady, Palamon wins the lady despite his defeat in battle, and Emilia secures as husband the man who loves her best and, incidentally the man who loves her first. It is no wonder that Theseus at the end of the play speaks of men as the playthings of the gods and decides to give up the attempt to understand their mysterious ways:

> with you leave dispute
> That are above our question.

We are left with the question of why Shakespeare in his last four or five plays introduced such scenes. The first and most obvious reason, as many critics have suggested, is that the use of Blackfriars made possible more spectacular scenes than the Globe had done, even though these plays were also staged at the Globe. Two of them were seen by Simon Forman there; *Henry VIII* was certainly staged there, and *The Tempest* may well have been. But it is difficult to imagine the masque in *The Tempest* being done adequately except in a covered theatre.

The second reason which has been advanced is the popularity of court masques in the reign of James I and the wish of the King's Players to cater for the fashionable taste. (There may even have been the possibility of using costumes which had already seen service at court). Against this it must be admitted that there were plenty of masques, or entertainments of a masque-like character, at the court of Queen Elizabeth and, moreover, that some Elizabethan dramatists introduced such entertainments into their plays. It is true that Jacobean masques were often concerned with divine or supernatural characters, and this may have encouraged Shakespeare to follow suit.

He may also have been influenced by the kind of material he was dramatizing. It would have been clearly wrong to have introduced theophanies in plays set in the Christian era. One cannot imagine the appearance of God to Richard III, to Richard II, or even to the saintly Henry VI. Viola and Beatrice were too self-seliant for divine revelations, and in the comedies written in the sixteenth century things work out happily without the need of divine intervention. Ghosts and apparitions influence the action of *Hamlet* and *Macbeth*. Despite Albany's prayer for direct intervention and his confidence that Cornwall's death was a sign that the gods had indeed punished the sinners, they do not prevent the death of Cordelia. Tragedy is possible only if the gods do not save human beings from the consequences of their actions. But when Shakespeare, influenced by the success of revivals of old romantic plays, went in search of similar material, happy endings were imperative, and they could be brought about only by giving the protagonists a second chance. Pericles has lost his wife and daughter: he regains them both by the help of Diana. Posthumus thinks he has murdered Imogen, but she is restored to him by the help of Jupiter. Leontes thinks he has killed Hermione and Perdita: he regains them both by the working out of Apollo's oracle. Prospero loses his dukedom and recovers it after fifteen years of exile. It is sometimes said, and often assumed, that the tragic view is truer to real life than the happy endings based on second chances and that Shakespeare was escaping from reality in his last plays: the tragic loading of Desdemona's bed is the inevitable result of Iago's villainy and Othello's credulity, whereas Hermione's recovery and Imogen's escape are improbable to say the least. But, as Calderón puts it, the worst is not always certain.

The pagan gods who watch over the actions of men in the last plays are a means of showing — as Professor William Elton thinks *King Lear* does not — that the universe is under the government of providence. This does not necessarily mean that Shakespeare's views on the matter underwent a change between 1605 and 1608; it means rather that in writing tragicomedy he was able to present a different emphasis, the more freely because of the pagan settings. But it may be noted that although one gets the impression of a theocentric universe in which things are working together for good — and although this was clearly intentional — nevertheless, the happy endings depend equally on the actions of the characters themselves. One could almost say that although the same endings could happen without divine intervention, they could not happen without positive virtuous action or repentance by the main characters. *Pericles*, as we have seen, is a special case, and *Henry VIII* and *The Two Noble Kinsmen* are not wholly Shakespeare's. But in the other three plays the happy endings depend on repentance and forgiveness.

Although there is no reason to doubt that Shakespeare was at least a nominal Christian, it is apparent from what has been said that the happy outcome is determined more by human character and conduct than by divine omniscience and omnipotence, especially in the plays which followed *Pericles*. Nevertheless, the theophanies are important, and they may be taken to signify that the virtuous actions of human beings are the best validation of the providential government of the world. The reunion of Pericles and Marina which makes him hear the music of the spheres, the resurrections of Thaisa and Hermione, the joy of reconciliation and forgiveness cemented by the marriage of children, are symbols of what might be, and should not be dismissed as sentimental day-dreaming by a dramatist declining into dotage.

NOTES

1. William Elton, *King Lear and the Gods* (Huntington Libr.: San Marino, Calif. 1966), p. 63.
2. Kenneth Muir, *Shakespeare as Collaborator* (Methuen: London 1960), p. 81.
3. In the Arden edition of *Cymbeline*, ed. J. M. Nosworthy (Methuen: London 1955), pp. xxiv-xxviii.
4. G. Wilson Knight defends it convincingly and brilliantly in *The Crown of Life* (Oxford University Press: London 1947). pp. 129-202.

6

The Betrayal of Shakespeare

The betrayal with which I am concerned in this article has
nothing to do with Shakespeare's private life — the seduction
of his friend by his mistress — for I now regard the *Sonnets* as
dramatic and possibly fictitious. I am concerned rather with
the betrayal of Shakespeare by his interpreters, both directors
and critics. I should make it clear that I admire many of both
kinds, the directors in the theatre for the last sixty years, and
the critics who have collectively increased our understanding
of Shakespeare's plays. Nevertheless, I believe that many
directors and critics, even good ones, have been guilty of
betraying Shakespeare by imposing on his work their limiting
theories.

Some mistakes are easily corrected and do little harm. One
famous historian declared that he did not know who had
written Shakespeare's plays, and the reason for his nescience
was that the poet was not mentioned in the book about the
athletic contests in the Cotswolds known as Dover's games.
But the only poets who figure in the book are the authors of
verses in praise of Dover, including Jonson and Drayton. It is
not surprising that Shakespeare did not contribute, since the
book was published twenty years after his death. Another
eminent historian, A. L. Rowse, recently declared that Ulysses'
great speech on order in *Troilus and Cressida* was an expression
of Shakespeare's personal convictions and nothing else. Now
Ulysses is a fox, a Machiavel, a manipulator, whose speeches are
never designed to enunciate truth but to sway opinion. One can
see him at work later in the same scene when he arranges to rig
the ballot, or later in the play when he pretends to Achilles that
the Greeks have begun to worship Ajax. Moreover, the speech
on Order, eloquent as it is, is a kind of anthology of what had
been written on the subject by Homer, Elyot, Hooker and in

the Homilies; and it is appropriate to the situation. The speech is the only one in the canon where the hierarchical organization of society is directly linked with cosmic order. Lear, soon afterwards, declares that the great image of authority is that a dog is obeyed in office; and in *All's Well that Ends Well* the King blows sky high the whole hierarchical system when he demonstrates that virtue, not birth, constitutes the true nobility. Ulysses' arguments, the King's defence of Helena, and Isabella's denunciation of proud man, 'Dressed in a little brief authority' are all appropriate to the characters speaking them and to the situations in which they are spoken.

Of course literary critics make the same kind of mistake. Bernard Shaw, the finest of all dramatic critics, argued that Shakespeare emerged from his tragic period, believing that life was a tale told by an idiot; and many critics have agreed with Swinburne that the essence of *King Lear* is contained in the lines:

> As flies to wanton boys are we to the gods:
> They kill us for their sport.

A short time afterwards, Gloucester, before attempting suicide, refers to the gods as 'kindly'. But why, we may ask, should either verdict be regarded as authorial? If Shakespeare wanted a spokesman, he would not have chosen that superstitious adulterer but one of his more sympathetic characters — Edgar, Kent, Cordelia, the Fool. Indeed, all these four do, at different times, act as a chorus. I am not suggesting that we can arrive at the meaning of a play by adding up the aphorisms of the sympathetic characters, but if we did that we should at least be less wrong than if we quoted only the remarks of the wicked and foolish.

Some critics distort the meaning of a play to conform with their own ideas. C. S. Lewis, in his brilliant lecture on *Hamlet*, showed that even the best critics differed about the character of the hero. He instanced Coleridge, Schlegel, Hazlitt and Goethe; he might have added Bradley, Freud, Knight, Knights and scores of others. If they all differ, Lewis asked, how can we regard the play as successful? His answer was that Hamlet had no specific character: he was Everyman, burdened with original sin and worried about the after-life. This is precisely what we should have expected Lewis to propound, since he was, in addition to being a fine literary critic, the author of several works of popular theology. He did not show, though he may have implied, that Hamlet's critics indulged in self-portraiture, or at least to be strongly influenced in their portraits of the Prince by their own prepossessions. Goethe's description of Hamlet, in *Wilhelm Meister*, is the portrait of a German Romantic hero. Coleridge, after arguing that Hamlet procrastinated from thought, losing the power of action in the energy of resolve, let the cat out of the bag by confessing, 'I have a smack of Hamlet myself, if I may say so'. He left 'Kubla Khan' and 'Christabel' as fragments, *Biographia Literaria* contains great criticism, but it is a structural mess, and his great philosophical work was left unwritten. Ernest Jones, the biographer of Freud, came to the not unexpected conclusion that the hero was suffering from an Oedipus Complex. A less orthodox analyst, Wertham, saved a boy from the electric chair by showing that he was in love with his mother, and that he had killed her with a bread-knife because matricide seemed to him less horrible than incest. The boy, we are told, differed from Hamlet because he had a low I.Q. and could not work off his guilty feelings by unpacking his heart with words. John Middleton Murry and Roy Walker, two Christian pacifists, concluded that Hamlet was wrong to kill Claudius, and this was also the conclusion of L.C. Knights and Eleanor Prosser. When I wrote my little book on the play, I therefore scrutinized my own experience and prejudices in the hope of avoiding the error of saddling Hamlet with my own views.[1] Would I, as a former city councillor, assume that Polonius was the key figure of the play? Would I, as a Fabian, assume that like Fabius in the Cathaginian War, Hamlet delayed for a while in order to strike more effectively? Would I, as a Christian existentialist, assume that Hamlet had to choose with anguish what course to follow, since on his choice depended the future of Denmark? Or would I, as the author of an article on 'The Uncomic Pun', declare that the real key to the understanding of the play was either the quibble on *conscience* in Hamlet's most famous soliloquy or the quibble on *acting*, activated by the performance of 'The Murder of Gonzago'?

The more we admire Shakespeare's works, the more we are

tempted to create the poet in our own image. This is a natural foible, if only because we would not like to think that he did not share our own enlightened opinions. Some months ago, I was assured by a professor from the Far East that Iago was Shakespeare's portrait of a British imperialist, revealed as such by his prejudices about the colour question. In the days before the rise of Hitler, the Social Democrat, Landauer, argued that Hamlet was a true democrat, on friendly terms with actors, soldiers, pirates and students, and that his tragedy was that he was far ahead of his time, before the creation of a democratic, equalitarian society. On the other side of the political fence, Warwick Bond, the editor of Lyly's works, came to the surprising conclusion that Sir John Falstaff, so loose in his morals, so fond of his liquor and so apt to cheat and steal, was Shakespeare's portrait of the British workingman. Some Soviet critics believe that Shakespeare regarded the early phase of capitalism with scathing contempt; others argue that he was somewhat to the left of centre of advanced bourgeois opinion. No doubt the followers of President Reagan and Mrs Thatcher will soon convince themselves that Shakespeare shared their views on the economy, and I look forward with some apprehension to a book on Shakespeare the Monetarist.

We are equally liable to saddle Shakespeare with our own religious convictions, or indeed, lack of convictions. How refreshing it would be to read a book by a Catholic, which did not conclude, with simulated surprise, that Shakespeare did not merely die a papist, as an early piece of gossip claimed, but that he lived a secret sympathizer with the old religion! And how refreshing it would be to read a book by a modern agnostic, which did not assume that the poet shared his views! The interpretation of individual plays often depends on the religious opinions of the critics. *Measure for Measure* has been interpreted as an allegory, the Duke representing God, Lucio Lucifer, and Elbow the arm of the law; or, alternatively, as a satire on the idea that the world was providentially governed. During my editorship of *Shakespeare Survey*, I published a number of articles on the play, with the certainty that after each one I would be deluged with indignant rejoinders by critics, repudiating its damnable errors.

We know that Shakespeare had a considerable knowledge of

the Bible, which he would have heard in church, week by week, in the Bishops' version. We know too that in later years he more frequently echoed the Geneva version, of which it is safe to assume he possessed a copy. But I do not believe that we can deduce his precise religious views from his works, since the views are always appropriate to the characters who utter them. Shakespeare apparently exhibits knowledge of the three concepts of Grace (Anglican, Calvinist, Catholic) in *Measure for Measure*. His acquaintance with four of Erasmus's works[2] has been taken to mean that he found that thinker congenial; but he seems to have been influenced in his later years by Montaigne. But we should remember that a man can be an admirer of an author without sharing his opinions. How many admirers of Eliot, Lawrence and Compton-Burnett share their religious, sexual and religious opinions?

It is the custom at Shakespeare conferences to split up into seminars to discuss his work from particular angles, in accordance with the dominant interests of the participants — bibliographical, textual, theatrical, marxist, feminist, psychoanalytical, symbolic. From those I have attended over the years I have usually learned a little which threw light on the plays; but I have become increasingly restless, as it has become apparent that many of the participants have subordinated their interest in Shakespeare, doubtless quite genuine, to their obsession with other matters. When feminists discuss Shakespeare's heroines, or Shakespeare and rape, they are more concerned with the exploitation of women over the centuries than with what Shakespeare actually said. Lisa Jardine, though herself highly critical of feminist criticism, declares in *Still Harping on Daughters* that the scene where Iago recites satirical verses to Desdemona would make the audience regard her as a temptress, a scold, a husband-beater and cuckolder, and she declares that Beatrice's shrewishness 'guarantees that her menfolk would either be emasculated or cuckolded'.[3]

Theologically-minded critics make similar mistakes. When a critic informs us that Shakespeare agreed with St Augustine that if Lucrece consented to her rape by Tarquin she did not deserve our sympathy, and if she did not consent, her suicide was a mortal sin, we begin to wonder if we are reading the same poem. When another critic assures us that all Shakespeare's tragic heroes fall through pride, we are bound to protest that although this applies accurately to Coriolanus, its fits Othello and Macbeth hardly at all. Theologically speaking, pride is the basic sin, but Shakespeare was not writing theology. He knew, of course, that there were seven deadly sins, but he knew equally that sloth and gluttony were unsuitable sins for tragic heroes, and that envy was more appropriate to villains.

All such approaches give us partial Shakespeares, and partial Shakespeares are distorted Shakespeares. I am not referring to the kind of misinterpretations we can all recognize — that Claudius is morally superior to his nephew, that Hermione represents Christ, Leontes the Jews, and Perdita the Church, that Cleopatra in her last hours followed the traditional principles laid down in devotional manuals for sin and preparation for death, or the attitude displayed in an article entitled 'That Four-flusher, Prospero', written by a docker in Liverpool. Such criticism carries its own antidote. I am referring rather to serious works of criticism, works of undoubted intelligence, from which we could all learn, but which are dangerous simply because the intelligence is used to impose a meaning, rather than to respond to the individuality of each of the plays. I am thinking of books which start with a plausible theory — about tragedy, comedy, farce, tragi-comedy, satire, pastoral — and then proceed to force each play into the theoretical pattern. It was this kind of book which made me assert that 'there is no such thing as Shakespearian tragedy: there are only Shakespearian tragedies'. In other words, they are all different; and to understand them and respond to them adequately, it is necessary to treasure what Blake calls their minute particulars. Sometimes, it must be admitted, the kind of book I have in mind is the result of a desperate search for a new topic.

Richard Levin, in his salutary book, *New Readings vs. Old Plays*, provides us with scores of examples of new and foolish interpretations of Elizabethan plays.[4] He divides these into several different categories. Many substitute a theme for the substance of a play. *A Midsummer Night's Dream* is concerned with reality and illusion; *Troilus and Cressida* is a philosophical contribution to the renaissance debate on honour. Other readings are based on the assumption that the surface meaning of a play is not the true meaning because of the underlying irony. The weddings that round off the comedies — Beatrice and Benedick, Rosalind and Orlando, Viola and Orsino, Portia and Bassanio — would all turn out to be misalliances. Then there are those readings in which it is assumed that we ought to use the ideas current in Shakespeare's day to correct the natural interpretation of the plays.

There is no easy remedy for the proliferation of this kind of criticism, for which universities are partly to blame. As Vincentio says, 'Novelty is only in request'. But it should always be remembered that a really new idea about one of Shakespeare's plays is unlikely to be true — the chance is not one in ten thousand. The other check on absurd novelties is the one proposed by Harriett Hawkins: when we conceive a theory, we ought, before we publish it, to compile a list of all the objections to it.

If our theatres were properly run, and if the plays were sensibly directed, as they sometimes are, stage productions would be an effective correction of critical eccentricities. But both in Britain and in other countries this is not so. This is partly because some of the best-known directors swallow trendy criticism, and because some of their own theories are equally perverse. There has, I think, been a change for the worse during my sixty years of play-going. I am well aware of the danger of relying on memories. One tends to be more favourably impressed by the first production of a play than by the thirtieth. One forgets the horrors and remembers only the successes. One was less disturbed in one's youth by deviations from the text because one did not know it so well. I must admit, moreover, that the general level of touring companies was dreadfully low. Benson was long past his best and his company was feeble in the twenties, Ben Greet by then was hammy and slapdash, and Bainton gave us some of the worst acting I can recall. The Stratford-upon-Avon company was mostly dull, and the productions were occasionally eccentric. The Duke in *The Merchant of Venice* played with a yo-yo during Portia's speech on mercy; a film of storm-clouds during the third act of *King Lear* caused hilarity when the same cloud kept recurring; and Shaw rewrote the last act of *Cymbeline*.

The great and glorious exception was the Old Vic. Here the

productions maintained a high integrity. This was partly because dozens of young actors were attracted to the theatre, despite the absurdly low salaries, because of the chance of playing leading roles to an intelligent and enthusiastic audience. Thorndike, Gielgud, Olivier, Redgrave, Evans, Richardson, Milton, Vosper and Swinley all made their names there. The other reason was that the directors made an honest and straightfoward attempt to present Shakespeare without gimmicks. The later productions were influenced by Granville-Barker's selfless *Prefaces,* in which his sole concern was to show how the plays could best be produced on the modern stage, with the minimum of deviation from the original performances. Barker regarded himself as a servant of Shakespeare, not as an exploiter. Nor was the Old Vic the only London theatre where one could see satisfying productions of Shakespeare. One need mention only the famous *Romeo and Juliet,* which starred four of the best Shakespearian actors of the present century, perhaps of any century: Evans, Ashcroft, Gielgud, Olivier.

In the post-war theatre there has been a radical change of attitude. We are now, for better or worse, in the age of Directors' Theatre. Its most obvious characteristic is that the director does not trust Shakespeare. He regards him as a great poet, but as a very incompetent playwright, whose work can be improved by cuts and additions. This attitude is a throw-back to the treatment of Shakespeare by the actors between 1660 (perhaps 1616) and the early years of the present century. Dryden genuinely believed that his perversion of *Troilus and Cressida* was a manifest improvement on Shakespeare's; and Nahum Tate believed that his *King Lear,* which ends with the marriage of Edgar and Cordelia, was better than the original. He explains why in his complacent preface. Garrick likewise thought that his *Romeo and Juliet* (in which the lovers converse in the tomb) and his rewriting of *The Winter's Tale* were laudible improvements. Modern directors are not usually so drastic in their alterations, at least with the major plays. But when John Barton, a director of genius, condensed the three parts of *Henry VI* into two plays, with the addition of several hundred lines of his own composition, the result was always interesting, but much less effective than the original trilogy.

The second characteristic of Directors' Shakespeare — and

this does not apply to the best of them — is that Shakespeare appears to be a means to an end, the end being their reputation, their glory, their advancement. It follows that their productions must appear to be new, so that critical attention will be directed away from the play itself, and away even from the acting, to directorial innovations. Only rarely do these innovations increase our understanding or enjoyment of the play.

The third characteristic is their determination to bring home to a supposedly illiterate audience the modern relevance of the play after three and a half centuries. The plays are really relevant because Shakespeare saw into the life of things, not because he was dramatizing the rise of fascism or the theories of Marx or Freud. He was not a forerunner of the theatre of the absurd, of the theatre of cruelty or of Brecht's political theatre. Shakespeare's *Macbeth* has no affinities with Ionesco; *King Lear* has no affinities with *End Game*, and still less with the plays of Artaud.[5].

I could illustrate these remarks from almost any Stratford season of the last twenty years. There was, for example, a *Measure for Measure* in which a hated actor-manager was supposed to be playing the part of the Duke, and he looked more like a demon-king than a bridegroom for Isabella. There was another production in which the Duke was old enough to be Isabella's grandfather, and a third production in which Mariana was discovered reclining on a haystack and drinking deep from a bottle of red wine. There was a recent *Taming of the Shrew*, which was performed as a piece of feminist propaganda, Petruchio exhibiting deep shame at Katharine's submission. There was Brook's famous production of *A Midsummer-Night's Dream*, brilliantly entertaining, but spoilt by a foolish programme note, alleging that Hippolyta was the most lecherous woman in all Shakespeare's works, and that Theseus was curing her of her perverted desires by making her alter-ago, Titania, have sexual relations with an ass.

Many other examples of directorial aberrations could be mentioned; but, in view of my criticisms, I must stress that I do not believe that there is only one right way to produce a play, and that there have been many first-rate productions at Stratford. I cannot imagine a better Lady Macbeth than Judi Dench's, a better Leontes than Gielgud's, a better Rosalind than Vanessa Redgrave's, a better Viola than Dorothy Tutin's, a better production of *Much Ado about Nothing* than the one in which Ashcroft and Gielgud played the leads.

One play with which I have been particularly concerned as director and editor is *Troilus and Cressida*. The play can be produced as a comical satire (as Oscar Campbell and Alice Walker advocated) or as a tragical satire. Either method is legitimate, especially as two productions in Shakespear's lifetime were different in emphasis.[6] After the most satisfying production of 1960, directed by Peter Hall and John Barton, described above,[7] later productions of the play have been a disappointment. They have all made Thersites, a scurrilous railer, to be Shakespeare's chief spokesman. The characters in the Greek camp were portrayed as pompous and feeble as Thersites later describes them, so that his satirical shafts seemed to be mere statements of fact. Achilles was apparently the effeminate partner in his relationship with a very masculine Patroclus. Even worse was the deliberate yawning by the actors during the great speeches of Ulysses, thus informing the audience that the boredom they suffered was shared by the director. The play ended with a scene Shakespeare did not write, in which a pox-ridden Thersites joined Pandarus for the epilogue. This was in 1976. Eight years later there was a better-balanced production, but there were some gross errors of taste, as when Agamemnon appeared, wearing a straw hat and carrying a frying-pan, as though the generalissimo had to cook his own breakfast.

The aberrations continue. In the 1982 production of *The Tempest* there was a fine performance by Derek Jacobi as Prospero, but for no apparent reason Ariel's farewell was omitted. In the same season there were some grotesque errors of judgement in the production of *King Lear*. In the storm scenes, Lear and the Fool, perched on a platform fixed to a pole, which rose out of the ground and then sank to ground level, naturally aroused laughter. The disappearance of the Fool after Act 3 was solved by the desperate expedient of having Lear kill him. Another mistake was a foolish cut. The dying Edmund, on hearing the story of his father's death, tells Edgar:

> This speech of yours hath moved me,

And shall perchance do good.

Although the director retained these lines, he perversely cut the ones in which Edmund acts on his unexpected feelings of remorse:

I pant for life. Some good I mean to do...

As the earlier lines were left intact, it was foolish to cut this speech which is necessary for our understanding of Edmund. What moves him to speak in the end is the sight of the bodies of Regan and Goneril. The bastard the deprived child, the disinherited, realizes that 'Edmund was beloved'.[8]

Dramatic critics often aid and abet the criminal activities of the directors, as when a *Sunday Times* critic, apparently without irony, remarked of a recent production of *The Comedy of Errors*:

> The idea I liked best of all was that of making the actors speak the verse pantomime style, with a blatant emphasis on simple rhythms and rhymes. This is some of the best verse speaking we have had at Stratford in recent years.

In America the situation is quite as bad, as one can see from the theatre reviews in recent numbers of *Shakespeare Quarterly*. In Alabama, for example, there was a performance of the Marowitz collage of *Hamlet* and a *Much Ado about Nothing* in Indian costume. At San Diego, *Much Ado* was set in the British Raj (as it had been at Stratford a few years ago). At Louisville, Fabian and Sir Andrew concealed themselves in barrels to remind the audience of Beckett; and the *Hamlet* there was based on the bad Quarto. The Cincinatti *Macbeth* was inspired by Kott. In Minneapolis there was 'a laughing cavalier' *Macbeth*. At Houston, Shylock was the hero and Antonio the villain. At Colorado, *All's Well that Ends Well* was played in Victorian costume. At Idaho *Much Ado* was given in the spirit of the roaring twenties, as it was in New Jersey the following year. The Synthaxis production of *The Tempest* featured a female Prospero, renamed Prospera. At Los Angeles, *Macbeth* was played in a post-holocaust setting. In San Francisco there was a *Hamlet* set in the gangster era of the twenties, with a nymphomaniac Orphelia. There was also a sado-masochistic

As You Like It and a pop-fantasy *Cymbeline*. At Seattle, *Measure for Measure* was set in the Vienna of Freud. At Champlain the citizens in *Corialanus* flaunted Solidarity banners. In *Much Ado*, set in 1814, Claudio is reported to have urinated on Benedick. Volumnia in *Coriolanus* was dressed in a Khaki shirt and trousers, and when she was not waving a rifle in the air, she was kicking the backsides of the tribunes. As a last horror we may mention the production of *Richard III* by the Australia National Theatre, in which the protagonist was depicted as an institutionalized madman reciting a condensed version of the play while seated on a toilet. The above is merely a summary of the responsible and even friendly reviews in *Shakespeare Quarterly.*

One of the keenest pleasures of playgoing is the realization that (in the words of Wordsworth):

> in spite of difference of soil and climate, of language and manners, of laws and customs, in spite of things silently gone out of mind and things violently destroyed, the Poet binds together by passion and knowledge the vast empire of human society, as it is spread over the whole earth, and over all time.
>
> (*Poetical Works*, ed. T. Hutchinson (1916), p. 938)

Directors of the kind we have been considering seem to lack faith in the power of great poetry to achieve this task. This denigrates the poets and insults their audiences throughout the world, who are quite capable of appreciating the differences between the world of 1600 and the world of today, and of understanding the insight into the human condition possessed by all great poets.

It may be said that although Shakespeare was confident that his powerful rhyme would outlast the monuments of princes, it is by no means certain that he had the same confidence about his plays, those fluid scripts. His project 'was to please'. He had to write parts for particular actors and to acquiesce in the mangling of his scripts for particular occasions. But to think of him as a mere purveyor of entertainment is to treat a nightingale as an exhibit in a poultry show. Those critics who regard him merely as the talented resident dramatist of the King's Men miss more than half of his quality.

How then are we to avoid the betrayal of Shakespeare?
There is no simple or single answer, but we can at least learn to
avoid the obvious pitfalls already discussed. We can avoid
forcing individual plays into the straitjacket of a general
theory, since each play's uniqueness is more important than its
generic resemblance to others. We can assume that the obvious
interpretation is probably the true one, since the plays were
written to be performed, and not before an audience of
scholars, theologians, or critics: but at the same time we must
allow for the presence of ambiguities and ironies which not all
members of an audience would have noticed. Above all, we can
avoid saddling Shakespeare with our own prepossessions, our
own complexes, our own prejudices. Keats, the most reliable
commentator on Shakespeare, singled out Negative Capability as the quality he possessed so enormously, and he later
remarked that 'the only means of strengthening one's intellect
is to make up one's mind about nothing — to let one's mind be
a thoroughfare for all thoughts. Not a select party'.[9] He was
writing of himself, but probably thinking of Shakespeare. 'A
thoroughfare for all thoughts' — for the thoughts suggested
by the tale he was dramatising, for the thoughts evoked by the
characters he had brought to life, who often surprised him and
sometimes appalled him. As a dramatist he never tried to prove
anything, never tried to illustrate a theory, although he stimu-
lates theories in his readers. As Proust remarked near the end
of his huge novel, 'A work in which there are theories is like an
object which still has its price-tag on it'. A dramatist raises
questions: it is not his business to provide answers. Perhaps
the man who composed the epitaph in Stratford church, in
which Shakespeare is compared not to Sophocles but to
Socrates, may have stumbled on the right idea; for Socrates,
notoriously, asked questions; and the only answers he gave
were in the guise of parables.

As for the critic, he can hardly make up his mind about
nothing or indulge, as critic, in negative capability; but he can
with advantage make his mind a thoroughfare for all thoughts.

NOTES

1. Kenneth Muir, *Shakespeare: Hamlet* (Arnold: London, 1963)
2. *Adagia, Colloquies, The Praise of Folly, De conscribendis epistolis.*
3. Lisa Jardine, *Still Harping on Daughters* (Harvester Press: Sussex, 1983), p. 120.
4. Richard Levin, *New Readings vs. Old Plays* (Chicago University Press, 1979).
5. Cf. 'The Irrelevance of Relevance', reprinted in *The Singularity of Shakespeare* (Liverpool University Press, 1977).
6. See above, Chapter 1. There is a brief stage-history of the play in my edition.
7. *Ibid.*
8. Moshinsky, whose television production of *All's Well that Ends Well* was perhaps the best in the B.B.C. series, absurdly misinterpreted *Cymbeline* when he declared that Imogen was not a good person in an evil world, but one who is nearly seduced by Iachimo. Happily Helen Mirren did not play the part like this.
9. Keats, *Letters:* 27.12.1817 and 24.9.1819.

7

Stendhal, Racine and Shakespeare

It is sometimes assumed that the idolatrous worship of Shakespeare was an essentially English phenomenon, one which was deplored by a clergyman in 1864, because a so-called Christian nation was paying 'almost idolatrous honour to the memory of a man who wrote so much that would not be tolerated in any decent domestic or social circle'. It is often suggested that until comparatively recently French critics were highly critical of Shakespeare, and French audiences uniformly hostile. Certainly Voltaire described *Hamlet* as 'a vulgar and barbarous drama, which would not be tolerated by the vilest populace of France or Italy'; and the summary he gave of the play shows him at his most disingenuous, or most forgetful:

> Hamlet becomes crazy in the second act, and his mistress become crazy in the third. The Prince slays the father of his mistress under the pretence of killing a rat, and the heroine throws herself into the river... Hamlet, his mother, and his father-in-law carouse on the stage; songs are sung at table; there is quarrelling, fighting, killing — one would imagine this piece to be the work of a drunken savage.

But although French readers and audiences, brought up on Corneille and Racine, did not easily accept plays written on entirely different principles, there were a number of enthusiastic admirers of Shakespeare throughout the nineteenth century. Victor Hugo's book, which no one would willingly read twice, is wildly and breathlessly enthusiastic about Shakespeare. Flaubert was a life-long idolator; as early as 1844 he exclaimed: 'Homer and Shakespeare, everything is there! The other poets, even the greatest, seem little beside them'.[1] He read his 'master, Shakespeare, with ever-increasing love'.[2] In

1851 he was equally enthusiastic: 'What a man! The greatest
only come up to his heels!'[3] He contrasted Molière, who was
always on the side of the majorities, with 'the great William'
who 'is on no one's side'.[4] Again and again Flaubert returned
to Shakespeare's power of creating characters, characters who
are a fusion of standard types and of 'new individuals who are
introduced into the human race.'[5] Much later, in 1878, Flaubert complained to Turgenev of Zola's confession in a review
that he had been bored by a performance of *Macbeth*. Turgenev
replied: I'm very much afraid that he has never read Shakespeare. That is an original stain in him which he'll never get rid
of'.[6] Neither Flaubert nor Turgenev was being fair to Zola,
who might have been forgiven for being bored by a performance in Italian of an adaptation of the play; but not to like
Shakespeare was apparently a sin for which there was no
forgiveness. The view is similar to Bradley's remark about his
Glasgow students, of whom he approved because they appreciated Shakespeare, which 'was the whole duty of man'.[7]

I have mentioned Hugo, Flaubert and Turgenev to show
that bardolatry was not an exclusively English heresy; and
when we turn to Stendhal's relations with Shakespeare we find
that he became equally a devotee. Not quite at first, as we can
see from the long and affectionate correspondence with his
sister Pauline. He spoke of her as beloved, sweet, charming and
divine; he assured her that he loved her more ardently than any
mistress he might have. Their marriage of true minds meant
that he was not merely her tutor in a prolonged correspondence course, but that he used the letters as a kind of journal in
which he could chart his own development and his rapidly
maturing taste. He passed on to Pauline his own enthusiasms
and discoveries, and he was delighted when he found that she
had arrived independently at the same opinion as he had
himself.

At first Racine was the god of his idolatry. In 1800 Stendhal
told Pauline: 'You should be able to read Racine — if you're
allowed'.[8] Not everyone regarded *Phèdre* as suitable reading
for a young girl. 'Read Racine without ceasing', he urges her
later;[9] and he tells her that every evening before going to bed,
however tired he is, he reads an act of one of Racine's plays, not
primarily for enjoyment, but in order to learn to speak

French.[10] He was pleased when Pauline disapproved of *Athalie*:

> *Athalie*, indeed, isn't Racine's best play; it is supremely immoral, in authorizing the priest to rebel against authority, and to massacre the magistrates; and it is precisely because of this major defect that the play pleases the Tartuffes of the century.[11]

Here one presumes that Stendhal — if he was not being ironical — was influenced more by anti-clericalism than by a Pauline belief (I refer to the saint not the sister) that one should always obey the powers that be.

Stendhal disliked *Iphigénie*. He remarked that Louis XIV was a great king in the opinion of blockheads, and *Iphigénie* their greatest tragedy.[12] By 1807 Stendhal was arguing that Racine was spoilt by his being a courtier:

> I sincerely despise Racine, in whose work I see all the platitudes he perpetrated at the court of Louis XIV. The custom of the court renders one incapable of feeling what is truly great.[13]

Stendhal had moved a long way in seven years. At first his tastes and critical views had been entirely classical. He believed strongly in adhering to the rules, in obeying the unities. He agreed with La Harpe that Racine was the first of all poets, past and present;[14] but he soon decided to free himself from the influence of La Harpe. He must, as he said, *délaharpiser son goût*.[15] His increasingly critical attitude to Racine and Corneille went side by side with an increasing awareness of Shakespeare's greatness. He advised Pauline to read Plutarch and Shakespeare, authors who depict things most resembling great events and tragic scenes.[16] He told her that the 'natural does not exist to such a degree in Corneille and Racine' as in Shakespeare.[17] He found in Shakespeare a mind as good or better than his own. His admiration, he declared, 'increases every day'.[18] Or, again, 'My passion for Shakespeare does not grow, because it couldn't.'[19] 'He is the most perfect image of nature. He isn't learned. There's no need to learn Greek. It's necessary to feel, not to be learned'.[20] Later on he recalled that a young colonel had said that since the Moscow campaign, *Iphigénie* was not so fine a tragedy. 'I prefer *Macbeth*'[21] One suspects that the young colonel was Stendhal himself.

By 1818 Stendhal could claim that he was 'a fanatical romantic — that is to say, I am for Shakespeare against Racine, and for Lord Byron against Boileau'.[22] There is some irony in this as Byron himself was for Pope, and against Wordsworth and Keats. In 1820 Stendhal suggested as an epitaph for himself '*Il adorait Shakespeare*'.[23] By this date he had reached step by step the position he first publicly expressed in *Racine et Shakespeare*, which first appeared in 1823 and in an enlarged edition two years later.

The writing of the tract was stimulated by two experiences. One was Stendhal's visit to London in 1821, when he saw Kean as Othello and Richard III and, incidentally, wrote an indignant letter to *The Theatrical Examiner*, complaining of alterations in the text.[24] The second stimulus was the hostile reception given to an English touring company which visited Paris in 1822. 'Down with Shakespeare! he was an aide-de-camp to the Duke of Wellington!' expressed the chauvinistic objections of the audience.[25]

Early in the tract, Stendhal declared that:[26]

> The whole dispute between Racine and Shakespeare is reduced to the question whether, by observing the unities of place and time, one can make plays which have a living interest for a nineteenth century audience, plays which make spectators weep and tremble.

He admits that obeying the unities is a French custom, a point he enforces with an effective pun — 'habitude profondément enracinée'.[27] But, in fact, his objection to plays written in the neo-classical style goes far beyond the question of the unities. He attacks the use of the obligatory rhymed Alexandrine in the plays of his contemporaries. 'In our days the Alexandrine is usually only a *cache-sottise*'.[28] He refers to several forgotten plays by Delavigne, Guiraud and Arnault, and complains that the pleasure they give is not really a *dramatic* one. 'The public . . . loves to hear the recitation of lofty sentiments in fine verse'.[29] The young, he declares, regard theatre-going as a mere accessory to the pleasure of reading; but a truly dramatic pleasure is aroused in the theatre when we forget our surroundings and the medium and succomb, if only at moments, to the illusion:[30]

> One of the things which is most hostile to the birth of these
> moments of illusion is admiration . . . for the beautiful verses of a
> tragedy.

He goes on to declare that 'these short moments of perfect
illusion are more often found in Shakespeare's tragedies than
in those of Racine'. He felt that English and Italian verse,
unlike Racine's, was able to say anything, and was therefore
not an obstacle to strictly dramatic beauties.[31] It should be
remembered that neo-classical critics did not believe that a
poet should say anything. Dr. Johnson, great critic as he was,
thought that in Lady Macbeth's invocation of the powers of
darkness she ought not to have been given such unpoetic
words as 'peep, 'blanket' and 'knife', as French critics complained, as Rymer had done, of Desdemona's handkerchief.
Nevertheless, although Stendhal was right to stress the advantages of being able to say anything, one cannot help being
uneasy at the drift of his argument; and this uneasiness is
increased by remarks made by Stendhal elsewhere. After
exclaiming that Shakespeare is 'the greatest Bard in [the]
world!', he adds 'And yet for me he is almost in prose.[32] In the
second edition of *Racine et Shakespeare* he quotes (inaccur-
ately) the words spoken by Macbeth when he sees the Ghost of
Banquo at the banquet: The table is full', and he asks: 'What
verse, what rhythm, could add to the beauty of such a phrase?[33]
He did not realize that Macbeth's words are the first half of a
regular blank verse line. Our uneasiness is further increased by
the fact that he singles out for praise those parts of Shakespeare's plays which are nearest to prose, and by his repeated
assertion that the poet's besetting fault was rhetoric.[34] He
praised a passage in *Henry V* as 'good Shakespeare without
rhetoric,' and the pedestrian opening of *As You Like It* for the
same reason.[35] Significantly, both passages are in prose.
Stendhal admitted that Shakespeare 'needed rhetoric to touch
people and make money, but rhetoric it is'.[36] Equally and
alarmingly significant is his description of *Antony and Cleopatra* as 'a poor tragedy without a trace of genius'[37] or his
dismissal of *The Tempest* as 'mediocre'[38] — two plays which
depend very much on their poetry.

It would not be true to say that Stendhall had no appreciation of Shakespeare's poetry. He singles out the passage about the temple-haunting martlet in the first act of *Macbeth*, a moment of repose and of dramatic irony just before the murder of Duncan, more profound (Stendhal suggests) than two of the most celebrated strokes in French classical tragedy —'*Qu'il mourût*' in *Horace* and '*Qui te l'a dit*' in *Andromaque*.[39] Yet, even here, it is Shakespeare's dramatic power which is being praised. Stendhal's knowledge of English seems to have been inadequate for him to appreciate poetic naunces, especially as he frequently read the plays in Le Tourneur's translation. He is more at home in writing of the dramatic effectiveness of individual scenes or of Shakespeare's powers of characterization. In his comments on individual plays he continually refers to the reality of the scenes and characters. Whereas other dramatists depict passions, Shakespeare depicts whole characters.[40] Although his characters use highly figurative language, it always speaks to the heart.[41] In five minutes one knows exactly what kind of woman Desdemona is: in this she differs from Corneille's characters:[42]

> We smile with pleasure to see in Shakespeare human nature as we feel it within ourselves. We identify with his characters... and tremble with them when a ghost appears.[43]

Othello is 'the most harrowing play' in all dramatic literature.[44] Although it was 'to please his English contemporaries' that Shakespeare wrote, he:

> left to natural objects their natural proportions; and that is why his colossal statue appears to us larger every day, whereas the little monuments of poets who seek to paint nature while flattering the affectations of the moment correspondingly diminish in size.[45]

Brulard, Stendhal's persona, spoke of his 'adoration for the tragic and simple truth of Shakespeare when contrasted with the bombastic puerility of Voltaire'.[46] So Stendhal admonishes himself to 'imitate Shakespeare — or rather nature'.[47] But he was well aware of the ambiguity of the classical precept: imitate nature.

> Every work of art is a beautiful falsehood (*un beau mensonge*).

Every writer knows this well. Nothing is more ridiculous than this advice given by the worldly wise: Imitate Nature.[48]

For how one imitates nature depends on the expectations of one's audience. Stendhal, who had only the haziest knowledge of the Elizabethan theatre, declared that Shakespeare:

> sought to please the country gentlemen who [as a result of the Wars of the Roses] were still blunt and uncultivated. Racine, on the other hand, sought the applause of polished courtiers who, following the code of manners established by the Marquis de Vardes, wished to please the King and earn the approval of the ladies. *Imitate Nature* is therefore meaningless advice.[49]

Stendhal continually contrasts Shakespeare's method with that of other dramatists, in particular with regard to his truthfulness. Even though art is a beautiful falsehood, Shakespeare, he seems to suggest, is an exception to the generalization.

> Among other tragic writers, the style and general colour of the dialogue, the distribution and economy of the various parts, are their principal aims: for Shakespeare it is the truth, and the strength of the imitation.[50]

Stendhal blames Alfieri's delicacy which prevents his characters from going into frank details: 'As a result we are never rent with terror as we are with Shakespeare's plays.'[51] Or again, he declares:

> for effeminate souls, blighted by study of Greek ... the masculine poetry of Shakespeare, which shows without flinching the evils of life, is physically unendurable.[52]

He notices the pure joy in Shakespeare's comedies, the characters in them who are animated by happy gaiety. 'Far from laughing at them, we sympathize with so delightful a state'.[53] He writes of the way events in Shakespeare's plays always spring from character[54] — a view which would find few adherents today. It would be nearer the truth to say that Shakespeare's characters are created to fit the actions demanded by the plot, though even this is a gross simplification.

When Stendhal praises the portrait of Imogen,[55] it is not because of the poetry she speaks or of the poetry she inspires in her husband, her brothers and Iachimo, but because of her behaviour in adversity:

> What produces in us the sensation of pure grace in Imogen, is that she laments without accusing anyone.[56]

Even in his most rhapsodic passages about Shakespeare, Stendhal says nothing about the poetry in which his comprehensive vision of life is expressed:

> How he flows like a river which overflows its banks and bears all before it!... How grand is his manner of painting! It is the whole of Nature. I feel ceaselessly for this great man the tenderest love and the liveliest admiration.[57]

Perhaps the strongest expression of that admiration is to be found in his journal in 1811, where he contrasts the great writers of the past with the lesser writers of the present and wonders how he could ever learn to carry on a conversation in the Elysian Fields with Shakespeare, 'quel dio ignoto',[58] Molière and the others. Shakespeare 'the unknown god' — bardolatry could hardly go any further. One is reminded of Flaubert's similar fear: 'I think that if I saw Shakespeare in person, I should die of fear'.[59]

Despite Stendhal's enthusiasm, we are driven to wonder with the late Professor Axelrad whether the author of *Racine et Shakespeare* 'understood at all what Shakespeare stands for and the reasons for his enduring fame'.[60] Of course Stendhal genuinely admired some of Shakespeare's real qualities, but it was an opponent of all that Racine and his disciples stood for that Shakespeare figures in *Racine et Shakespeare*, the violator of the unities, the poet who could say anything, the dramatist whose poetry did not destroy the illusion of reality. Although Stendhal did read Shakespeare in the original, he also read and annotated Le Tourneur's prose translation. Indeed, he would really have preferred a prose Shakespeare. In 1822, for example, he was advocating the writing of tragedy in prose and the following of Shakespeare's methods.[61] Again, in *Racine et Shakespeare* he declared that tragedies should be written in prose;[62] and he remarked that Mademoiselle Mars was better at delivering prose than verse, without regarding this as a limitation of her ability as an actress.[63]

In some ways Stendhal was a forerunner of Ibsen, who after writing *Brand*, turned his back on verse for reasons he explained in a letter.[64] Art forms die out; verse had done immense harm to the art of the theatre, and so for twelve years he had devoted himself to the more difficult task of imaginative creation in the plain unvarnished speech of reality. If one reads the English poetic dramas of the eighteenth and nineteenth centuries, one is bound to agree with Ibsen that they belonged to a moribund tradition: Addison, Thompson, Johnson, Gray, Wordsworth, Coleridge, Shelley, Keats, Browning, Tennyson, Swinburne, Hopkins, Morris, Arnold, all tried their hands at poetic dramas, and not one of them has survived in the theatre. The same thing could be said about the poetic plays being written in France at the beginning of the nineteenth century. Is even Hugo part of the living theatre?

Although Stendhal declared that he loved Racine passionately,[65] he believed nevertheless that there was 'a fight to the death' between the tragic system of Racine and that of Shakespeare.[66] As applied to the theatrical situation in 1822, the belief had some justification; but Stendhal sometimes used Shakespeare, in the heat of the controversy, as a stick to beat not merely Racine's imitators, but the master himself.

It is surely not true to suggest that the more beautiful the poetry, and the more beautifully it is delivered, the less dramatic the performance becomes, or that the dramatic illusion is continually shattered by our consciousness of the art employed by the poet. Similar fears have been entertained by British directors of Shakespeare who tried for a while to make the actors speak the lines as though they were prose. One director tried to enforce this policy by having the whole script of *Antony and Cleopatra* typed out as prose. Even directors who like their cast to speak the blank verse as verse sometimes do their best to conceal the fact that many passages in Shakespeare's mature plays are rhymed; and it is not unknown for French actors to hurry over the rhyme of a Racinean Alexandrine, as though it were slightly improper. But these are aberrations. It is surely quite wrong to regard poetry as the enemy of drama. Although people in real life do not talk like Athalie, Cleopatra or Macbeth, in the theatre an audience can be dramatically excited and caught up in the illusion. The member of an audience in the United States who shot the actor playing Iago, and the Russian coal miner who leapt up and shouted 'Shooting's too good for such a bastard!' were not prevented by the verse from total absorption in the drama. When we listen to Athalie recounting her dream of Jezabel, we can appreciate the beauty of the verse and the genius of the actress, at the same time as we give ourselves up to the dramatic situation. There is the same complexity of response when we listen to an actor delivering one of Hamlet's soliloquies. The audience's familiarity with the lines adds to the actor's difficulties, but Racine and Shakespeare can hardly be blamed for that.

When Charlotte Brontë described a performance by Rachel as Phèdre, it is noteworthy that her reactions, or those of the heroine of *Villette,* are those of a spectator, moved, excited, horrified and shocked, not that of a culture-vulture listening to a poetry recital:

I had seen acting before, but never anything like this.
Never anything which astonished Hope and hushed Desire;
which outstripped Impulse and paled Conception; which,
instead of merely irritating imagination with the thought
of what *might* be done, at the same time fevering the nerves
because it was *not* done, disclosed power like a deep,
swollen winter river, thundering in cataract, and bearing
the soul, like a life, on the steep and steely sweep of
its descent.[67]

But even poets have sometimes feared that poetry was a dramatic liability. T. S. Eliot once expressed the hope that the audience would not realize that one of his plays was in verse, since he believed that a natural response to poetic drama was warped by literary snobbery and the self-satisfaction engendered by being bored in a worthy cause. But if we are bored by *The Elder Statesman,* it is not because it is too poetical, but because it isn't poetical enough.

Stendhal, then, despite his glorification of Shakespeare,

misunderstood his methods in several important respects. Along with his English contemporaries, he was ignorant of Elizabethan stage conventions and of their effect on the plays, especially on their method of characterization. Moreover, he did not realize that the rounded nature of Shakespeare's characters is the result of the 'secret impressions' set in motion by the poet, to use Maurice Morgann's phrase.[68] The different views expressed about a character, which are frequently conflicting, and sometimes the apparent inconsistencies in a character's actions, give a more lifelike effect than consistency would do. One of the most effective moments in *Athalie* is when the ruthless and evil queen, beholding the boy who reminds her of her lost innocence, is, to her own astonishment, moved by pity.

A more serious weakness is Stendhal's use of 'rhetoric' in a perjorative sense. He presumably means that Shakespeare sometimes writes in an artificial style, too far removed from the language of men; that his characters sometimes seem to orate to each other, as Corneille's notoriously do; that we become too conscious of the art and miss what Keats called 'the true voice of feeling'. We may admit that these strictures are applicable to Shakespeare's earliest plays, but if we read his works in chronological order, we become aware that the verse becomes progressively less stilted and his language more colloquial; that he tends to avoid the more artificial figures of rhetoric; and that the lines are no longer end-stopped. But it would be wrong to suppose that he abandoned rhetoric in the way that Berowne forswears 'three-piled hyperboles, silken terms precise'.[69] There are over a hundred figures of rhetoric, and most of them Shakespeare continued to use to the end of his career.[70] The idea that he abandoned rhetoric is simply due to the greater subtlety with which he used rhetorical figures, using art to conceal his art. We are made to believe — we are conned into believing — that his characters converse with each other, that they are not letting off set speeches.

If one examines any of Shakespeare's mature plays, one finds rhetorical devices used with practised skill. There is some affinity between the art of the dramatist and the art of the barrister: Shakespeare, it may be said, appears as the poet for the defence. In *Troilus and Cressida, Julius Caesar* and

Coriolanus, plays which contain set orations, the obvious rhetoric is perfectly appropriate both to the characters and to the situations. We may mention the debates in the Greek camp and the Trojan council chamber, the speeches at Caesar's funeral by Brutus and Antony, and Volumnia's appeal to her son to spare Rome, or the eulogy of Coriolanus by Cominius. In *Hamlet* the rhymed verse of *The Mousetrap* and the deliberately inflated verse of the speeches from the Dido play contrast in their different ways, not merely with the prose of Hamlet's advice to the players and the long prose scene of Act 2 Scene 2, but equally with the colloquial blank verse of Hamlet's second and third soliloquies. Extracted from the play these soliloquies might seem to be unduly rhetorical, but in their context they seem to be the natural thoughts of a tortured man. Less obviously the balanced rhetorical style of Claudius' first speech contrasts with the passionate outburst of Hamlet's first soliloquy. But we hardly realize that the passion is expressed in a series of rhetorical devices.

When we consider that Stendhal thought that *Antony and Cleopatra* was destitute of genius and that *The Tempest* was only mediocre, we are bound to wonder whether his real objection was not to rhetoric but to poetry, that he demanded tragedies in prose because he was suspicious of poetry. As Aristotle pointed out, imagery is one of the chief qualities by which we can recognize a poet, and when Stendhal asked Pauline to make a list of Shakespeare's faults, he himself mentioned imagery as one of them:

> He makes his characters speak in images. This method is brilliant; and it impresses people because they understand them perfectly.[71]

The implication is that the people's taste is bad. Racine uses imagery less than any other great poet, and it is clear that Stendhal had not completely purged his taste of La Harpe.

Most of Stendhal's discussion of Shakespeare belongs to the years immediately preceding the publication of *Racine et Shakespeare*, but it should not be thought that his admiration declined when the name of his idol ceased to be a battle-cry. Some of his most enthusiastic remarks were written in his journal, and were not intended for publication. 'In speaking of other poets', he wrote, 'there is always an alloy in one's esteem: with him I always feel a thousand times more than I express.[72]

We may suggest in conclusion that Stendahl found in Shakespeare what he needed. It was not the whole of Shakespeare, but his truth to life, his refusal to flinch from unpalatable truths, his unequalled range of characters, his fundamental realism beneath the *beau mensonge* of art, were qualities that Stendhal himself sought to emulate in *La Chartreuse de Parme* and *Le Rouge et Le Noir*.

NOTES

1. Letter from Gustave Flaubert, 7.6.1844. *Correspondance,* (Conard: Paris, 1926-33), I.154.
2. *Ibid.,* 13.8.1845 (I.187).
3. *Ibid.,* 25.1.1852 (II.360).
4. *Ibid.,* 2.11.1852 (III.47).
5. *Ibid.,* 25.9.1852 (III.31).
6. Ivan Turgenev, *Works and Letters* (Moscow, 1968), XXVIII. 256.
7. Cited K. Cooke, A.C. Bradley (Oxford, 1972), p. 37.
8. Stendhal, *Correspondance,* (Pléiade ed.), I.2.
9. *Ibid.,* I.29, 38.
10. *Ibid.,* I. 44-5.
11. *Ibid.,* I.55.
12. *Ibid.,* I.131.
13. *Ibid.,* I.353.
14. Stendhal, *Oeuvres Complètes,* ed. V. del Litto and E. Abravanel 50 vols., Geneva, 1968-74), XXXVII.12.
15. *Ibid.,* XXVIII.195.
16. *Correspondance,* I.163.
17. *Oeuvres,* XXXIII.143.
18. *Ibid.,* XXXIII.248.
19. *Correspondance,* I.578.
20. *Oeuvres,* XXXIII.248.
21. *Ibid.,* XLI.207.
22. *Correspondance,* I.909.
23. *Oeuvres,* XXXVI.72.
24. *Correspondance,* II.1.
25. *Oeuvres,* XXXVII.141.

26. *Ibid.*, XXXVII.9.
27. *Ibid.*, XXXVII.9.
28. *Ibid.*, XXXVII.3.
29. *Ibid.*, XXXVII.8.
30. *Ibid.*, XXXVII.19.
31. *Ibid.*, XXXVII.86.
32. *Ibid.*, XXVII.265.
33. *Ibid.*, XXXVII.146.
34. *Ibid.*, XLIX.177.
35. *Ibid.*, XLIX.179.
36. *Ibid.*, XLIX.177.
37. *Ibid.*, XLIX.175.
38. *Ibid.*, XXXVII.96.
39. *Ibid.*, XXVIII.264.
40. *Ibid.*, XXXIV.65.
41. *Ibid.*, XXXIV.65.
42. *Ibid.*, XXXIV.336.
43. *Ibid.*, XXXIII.296.
44. *Ibid.*, XXIII.404.
45. *Ibid.*, XXVI.105.
46. *Ibid.*, XXI.147.
47. *Ibid.*, XXXIII.297.
48. *Ibid.*, XLVI.223.
49. *Ibid.*, XLVI.223.
50. *Ibid.*, XIV.185.
51. *Ibid.*, XXVIII.137.
52. *Ibid.*, XXXV.119.
53. *Ibid.*, XXXV.51.
54. *Ibid.*, XXIX.160.
55. *Ibid.*, XXXIV.321.
56. *Ibid.*, XXXVI.323.
57. *Ibid.*, XXVIII.273
58. *Ibid.*, XXX.101.
59. Flaubert, *Correspondance*, III.45.
60. *Shakespeare Survey 16*, pp. 53-6.
61. *Oeuvres*, XLVI.68.
62. *Ibid.*, XXXVII.3.
63. *Ibid.*, XXXVII.248.
64. Letter to Lucie Wolf (25.5.1883).
65. Cf. n.9.
66. *Oeuvres*, XXXV.127.
67. Charlotte Brontë, *Villette*, Chapter 23.
68. Maurice Morgann, *Shakespearian Criticism*, ed. Daniel A. Fineman (Oxford, 1972), pp. 146 ff.

69. *Love's Labour's Lost,* V.ii.307.
70. Sister Miriam Joseph, *Shakespeare's Use of the Arts of Language* (Columbia University Press; New York, 1947), *passim.*
71. *Correspondance,* I.235.
72. *Oeuvres,* XXVIII.273.

8
Shakespeare and Calderón

These two great dramatists seem at first sight to have little in common: Shakespeare essentially English, Calderón essentially Spanish; Shakespeare predominantly secular, Calderón Catholic, and even clerical. The contrast was underlined by Shelley, who spoke of the 'starry' and 'incomparable' *Autos* in which Calderón:

> had attempted to fulfil some of the high conditions of dramatic representation neglected by Shakespeare; such as the establishing a relation between drama and religion.

It is this feeling of a certain absence of religion in Shakespeare's plays which leads devout critics to supply the want by allegorizing them. But it is worth noticing that Shelley goes on to say that Calderón:

> omits the observation of conditions still more important, and more is lost than gained by a substitution of the rigidly-defined and ever-repeated idealisms of a distorted superstition for the living impersonations of the truth of human passion.[1]

How far is Shelley right in his assertion that Calderón's dramatic instincts were sometimes thwarted by his religious convictions? Did he sometimes substitute ideals for realities? We may attempt to answer these questions by a number of comparisons of plays where the two dramatists are concerned with similar material — the unreality of human life, love comedies, tragedies of wife-murder and treatments of the same theme.

Both dramatists wrote plays on the subject of Coriolanus, both wrote, in whole or in part, plays about Edward III, and both wrote on Henry VIII. We may therefore begin by a detailed comparison of *La cisma de Inglaterra* with *Henry VIII.*

1

Until recently the main comparative study of the two plays was A. A. Parker's well-known article published in 1948, and since reprinted in J. E. Varey's anthology (1973).[2] Parker's article is the only criticism of the play listed in Edward M. Wilson's chapter on Calderón's dramatic work.[3] Since then John Loftis, while not denying Parker's high estimate of Calderón's play, cogently argues that he was unfair to *Henry VIII*.[4] I believe that the verdicts of Parker and Loftis should undergo further scrutiny.

The two plays are to some extent conditioned by their dates, by the audiences for which they were written and by the convictions, or lack of convictions, of their respective authors. Writing only ten years after the death of Elizabeth I, and at a time when the defects of her successor made her more valued than she had been in the last years of her reign, Shakespeare and Fletcher (if he was the joint author)[5] could not depict her as illegitimate, or her mother, Anne Boleyn, as an incestuous and adulterous wife. Nor could they openly deplore the Anglican religious settlement, nor pretend that the martyrs depicted in Foxe's *Acts and Monuments* deserved their fate. Calderón, on the other hand, a Catholic in a Catholic country, a priest, moreover, writing a play for performance before the king, at a time when Spain and England were at war,[6] was bound to take a different view. The divorce of Katherine, the proximate cause of the Reformation in England, meant that Anne was regarded in Spain as heretical and evil. She had been executed on the charge that she had committed adultery with several men, including her own brother, and Catholic propagandists added the accusation that she was Henry's own daughter. Calderón did not make use of these scandals because he believed that the sins of the flesh were less damnable than those of the spirit — her vaulting ambition and her heresy. Her relations with Carlos took place before her meeting with the

King, and she is condemned more for infidelity than for fornication, though she appears to be willing to contemplate adultery with Carlos, and their amorous conversation is overheard by the King. In one respect, however, Calderón blackens her character: she sends poison to Catherine, but whether the recipient dies as a result or from natural causes is not revealed. Even Parker admits that the poisoning was dramatically unnecessary; it is as silly as Thackeray's pretence that Becky, at the end of *Vanity Fair,* was guilty of murder.

Calderón's portrait of Anne therefore contrasts with Shakespeare's, as one would expect from one writing in the climate of the Counter-reformation. He also blackens Wolsey, making him the tempter who suggests the divorce to Henry and suggesting to Anne how she may become Queen. In the end, dismissed by the King, he is reduced to beggary, despairs and commits suicide — dies, that is, in mortal sin. On the other hand, Calderón's portrait of Henry is unexpectedly favourable. He omits some of the harsher traits of his source. The King falls into temptation because of his passion for Anne, repents as soon as he realizes Anne's true nature and tries to make amends by proclaiming Mary as his heir, in the knowledge that she will restore the true faith.

Parker admits that *La cisma de Inglaterra* is 'a travesty of history', but he points out that in both England and Spain the dramatist had freedom to alter the facts to suit a dramatic plan. Shakespeare (he might have said) switched the murder of Duncan to Macbeth's castle, he made Richard III die at the hands of Richmond, Hotspur at the hands of Hal. There is no reason why Calderón should not have an equal freedom in dramatizing the story of Henry's divorce. But one cannot help feeling that the alterations were made not primarily for dramatic reasons but in the interests of religious dogma. Calderón assumes, as he must, that the Reformation was a disaster, and that it was brought about by the King's passion for Anne, by Anne's ambition, by Wolsey's ambition and by his hatred for Catherine. Everything is reduced to its simplest terms; everything is black or white. It is nowhere admitted that the reformers had a valid or even a plausible case.

At the opening of the play the phantasm of Anne appears to Henry as a kind of evil angel, interrupting his confutation of

Luther. Wolsey is depicted as favouring the match between Henry and Anne, although, as Shakespeare reminds us, Wolsey objected to the marrige because Anne was a 'spleeny Lutheran'. By making her absolutely evil, Calderón runs the risk of lapsing from mature drama into a morality play.

One of the five principles governing the structure of the *comedia*, as outlined by Parker, is 'the subordination of the theme to a moral purpose through the principle of poetic justice'. The moral purpose of *La cisma* is to show that the English Reformation was wrong, and that it was brought about by the sinfulness of individuals and by the devil, working through Anne and Wolsey. Poetic justice is satisfied by the execution of Anne, the fall and suicide of Wolsey, and the determination of Mary to restore the old faith as soon as she gets the chance. Calderón even clings to the idea of poetic justice in relation to Catherine because she is rude and haughty to Wolsey. One may doubt whether poetic justice requires that impoliteness should be visited with divorce and death, as many readers of *King Lear* refuse to believe that Cordelia's conduct in the first scene, whether defined as tactlessness or self-respect, should be punished with the hangman's rope. Shakespeare depicts his Katherine as an innocent victim; but, as Parker declares, 'in the world of tragic human error that Calderón's play presents ... there is no such thing as innocent suffering'.

Catherine and Katherine are best contrasted in the speeches they make in their defence. Shakespeare's, superbly effective on the lips of great actresses from Sarah Siddons to Edith Evans, is closely based on the words given by Holinshed, some twenty lines being borrowed with the minimum of change, only enough to convert indifferent prose into great verse:

> Sir, I desire you do me right and justice,
> And to bestow your pity on me; for
> I am a most poor woman, and a stranger,
> Born out of your dominions; having here
> No judge indifferent, nor no more assurance
> Of equal friendship and proceeding. Alas sir,
> In what have I offended you? What cause
> Hath my behaviour given to your displeasure

That thus you should proceed to put me off,
And take your good grace from me? Heaven witness,
I have been to you a true and humble wife,
At all times to your will conformable,
Ever in fear to kindle your dislike,
Yea, subject to your countenance, glad or sorry
As I saw it inclined: when was the hour
I ever contradicted your desire,
Or made it not mine too? Or which of your friends
Have I not strove to love, although I knew
He were mine enemy? What friend of mine
That had to him derived your anger, did I
Continue in my liking? Nay, gave notice
He was from thence discharged? Sir, call to mind
That I have been your wife, in this obedience,
Upward of twenty years, and have been blest
With many children by you: if in the course
And process of this time you can report,
And prove it too, against mine honour aught,
My bond to wedlock or my love and duty,
Against your sacred person, in God's name,
Turn me away, and let the foul'st contempt
Shut door upon me, and so give me up
To the sharp'st kind of justice. Please you, sir,
The king, your father, was reputed for
A prince most prudent, of an excellent
And unmatch'd wit and judgement: Ferdinand,
My father, king of Spain, was reckon'd one
The wisest prince that there had reign'd by many
A year before: it is not to be question'd
That they had gathered a wise council to them
Of every realm, that did debate this business,
Who deem'd our marriage lawful: wherefore I humbly
Beseech you, sir, to spare me, till I may
Be by my friends in Spain advised, whose counsel
I will implore: if not, i'the name of God,
Your pleasure be fulfill'd!

After some bitter exchanges with Wolsey, Katherine leaves
the court and the King bears witness to her nobility and virtue.
This is the corresponding speech in *La cisma de Inglaterra*:

Deign, Sire, to hear me,

If perchance my sobs will give me leave
To utter a few words. Henry, my king,
My lord, my master, my beloved husband —
For I still wish to call you by that name
In which I adore the sacrament of marriage —
That which afflicts me is not that I am banished
From the royal throne, is not to see my brow
Robbed of the crown, and not to see the sceptre
Snapped in my hand; I leave it to Ambition
To mourn vain trophies Death will snatch from us
Sooner or later; but I'm desolate
To find me out of favour, to suppose
I am a cause of grief, and brought you, Sire —
I know not how — to such a cruel decision.
And if you're not convinced that I'm sincere,
Then put me in a prison where my eyes
Cannot behold the sweet light of the sky;
Or set me in a forest where wild beasts
Are all my company; or in the midst
O'th' sea upon a barren rock. Yea, Sire,
Wherever it is, I yet could be content,
Provided that I knew that I had found
Grace in your sight, and that I could still call you
Husband. However I am willing to comply
With all your wishes, I would not regret
At being so far from you, could I be tranquil
In knowing that your conduct was the pretext
For further troubles? You, the most Christian king,
You so wise, and so religious, you so long
The pillar of the church, you who confounded
With so much wisdom Luther's heresies,
You could throw doubt upon the sunshine! I
Am less wise than you; but when it's matters
Of faith that are in question, I am certain
That he who sails upon the sea will come
To a disastrous end if he removes
The pilot from the wheel. Schisms and heresies
Present themselves under a pious mask,
But soon reveal themselves in their true colours.
Take care, my lord, to shun that slippery slope
On which a fall is certain in the end.
The sovereign pontiff is God's deputy,
And, even as God himself, he can do all.

This is revealed to me, and this I know.
To him I appeal, and I will go to Rome
To ask for justice. I could retire to Spain,
Where the victorious Charles would give me aid;
But this I want not, and do not invoke.
I do not seek for vengeance; if I had
Ever solicited revenge on you,
My heart, my very heart, would shield you then,
For I would call on it the destined blows.
Nor do I wish to take the veil, retire
Into a convent, for, if I am married,
It would be vain to seek a different state.
So I will stay, Sire, in a royal palace,
Under a roof where you sometimes have dwelt;
And when I die there everyone will know
That I have always loved you, recognized
You as my master, as my wealth, my king,
My husband. What! You're going? But, alas,
If I should see you vexed, it would be better
Not to see you; better for me to die
And spare you new annoyances. Alas!
Unhappy that I am, the sun which lit me
Has disappeared, and I am left in darkness.

It is important to notice the great difference between the scenes in which these speeches are spoken. Shakespeare has a much more elaborate setting with a lot of pageantry, with two cardinals, an archbishop and four bishops, a number of officials and noblemen on the stage, and the proceedings are authorized by a commission from Rome. Calderón has none of this pageantry; there is no authority from the Pope, and the King pronounces the divorce as an act of dictation. Shakespeare's Henry, with apparent sincerity, pays tribute to Katherine's sweet gentleness and her saint-like meekness, describing her as a sweet bedfellow and 'the queen of earthly queens'. Calderón's Henry, on the other hand, although admitting while she is present that she is a model of virtue, one whom he loves with all his soul, has earlier made it clear that he has ceased to love her, and that he regards her with aversion. Shakespeare's Katherine stresses the length of her marriage and the wisdom of their parents in making sure that it would be valid. Calderón's

Catherine mentions the sacrament of marriage, and the climax of her speech is a warning against schisms and heresies. Katherine blames Wolsey for the divorce proceedings; Catherine pleads with Wolsey to give the King good counsel, but she lacks the spirit and righteous indignation of Shakespeare's character. Calderón focusses attention on the religious issue; at this point in the play Shakespeare ignores the religious question and concentrates on the spectacle of suffering innocence. In Katherine's final scene, however, there is an endearing mixture of religious resignation and queenly pride, outraged by the lack of respect shown by a messenger.

Calderón had every right, of course, to subordinate character to theme, even though this meant a certain dramatic loss. From his point of view it was desirable to suppress the commission from Rome; but one cannot help thinking that he could have stuck to his theme without sacrifice of drama, if he had made Catherine argue for the validity of the marriage and attack Wolsey. Neither woman refers to Anne, as though they were ignorant of the King's intentions, and Catherine actually sends Anne to plead with the King on her behalf.

According to Parker the superiority of Calderón's play to *Henry VIII* 'in conception and construction is overwhelming,'[7] and Loftis, although showing that Parker has undervalued *Henry VIII*, does not question his valuation of *La cisma de Inglaterra*. One should not, of course, condemn Calderón because his method differs completely from that of the best Elizabethan and Jacobean dramatists, but we may suggest that the play is not as faultless as Parker pretends when he declares that it is:

> marvellously constructed, its three acts presenting an exposition, a development, and a denouement that are tightly knit together. There is no ambiguity of tone, no shifting centre of interest and no uncertainty of aim (as in *Henry VIII*) ... the action is compressed and its course relentlessly swift.

I will return later to the question of ambiguity, which is a crucial difference between Calderón and Shakespeare. At this point I would merely question whether the play is as well constructed as Parker suggests. In the first place, the exposition seems somewhat clumsy: after the appearance of Anne's *figura*, the King is given a long speech to provide the audience with necessary information. Calderón endeavours, but not quite successfully, to make this information dramatic by linking it with the King's agitation. Then again, in the last act the King hides behind the arras, without plausible motivation, so that he can overhear the conversation between Anne and Carlos. Parker may be right to believe that action is more important than characterization, but the action must strike the audience as natural and not merely, as in this case, a device to cut corners.

The action of the play is, indeed, swift. Calderón crowds into the last act enough material to fill a complete play, and events are so accelerated that the audience has not enough time for the action to be fully effective. Carlos determines to confront Anne; Wolsey dismisses the soldiers' petitions and asks Anne to reward him with the position he seeks; Anne gratuitously inserts poison in the King's letter to Catherine and asks the King to punish Wolsey, which he does forthwith, not merely dismissing him but telling the returned soldiers to ransack his property; the poisoned letter is delivered, though we are not told if this is the cause of her death; the King overhears the conversation between Anne and Carlos, and forthwith orders her execution — the historical Henry orders a trial on more serious charges; Mary arrives to announce the death of Katherine — the King repents of his infidelity and proclaims Mary as his heir. She ascends the throne, triumphing over the corpse of Anne; she swears not to alter the country's religion, nor to restore ecclesiastical property, but it is plain that she has no intention of keeping her oath, and that we are supposed to approve of her deceit. The speed of this act is such that Anne's father agrees without hesitation to supervize her execution. The use of Anne's corpse as a kind of stepping-stone, though symbolically interesting, strains our credulity and is, I think, morally repugnant. We are not told whether Mary knows of Anne's fornication and intended adultery.

As we have seen, Parker compliments Calderón on his lack of ambiguity, but it may be suggested that this is a moral rather than an aesthetic or dramatic, virtue. Shakespeare flaunts the ambiguity of *Henry VIII*. Henry, Parker says, is shown to be wrong in his conduct, and yet we are asked to believe that the fact that he gets his way in divorcing Katherine and marrying Anne is 'a matter for congratulation to everybody'. Such a confused tone, Parker thinks, 'is incompatible with the depth and seriousness that should characterize poetic drama when it sets out to move on as high a level as this play does'. Or, as James Smith, quoted by Parker, remarks, the characters 'lack the moral dimension which characterizes history'. Parker complains that 'the final vision of Elizabethan England ... is not a conclusion that inevitably follows from the interpretation and treatment of the theme'. If, however, the theme is the way by which Protestantism was established in England, a form of Christianity by which God would be truly known, then the prophecy of Cranmer would be a fitting climax to the play — if not to readers who deplore the Reformation. In the eyes of Shakespeare, Providence, working through sinful human beings, with inevitably mixed motives, brings about the desired result. What other instruments has Providence ever had?

Just as Calderón omits the birth of Elizabeth, so Shakespeare stops at the point of Anne's triumph. But his audience would be perfectly aware that the falls of Buckingham, Wolsey and Katherine in the course of the play would have been followed, if there had been a sequel, by the falls of Anne, Cromwell and Cranmer. When Parker describes Cranmer's humility as 'political servility rather than religious meekness', he is not describing Shakespeare's character, nor even the historical character who dies ultimately for his beliefs.

It is important to realize that the ambiguity of which Parker complains is regarded by most modern critics of Shakespeare as a positive quality rather than a cowardice caused by lack of conviction. It is one aspect of the negative capability described by Keats as 'the power of being in uncertainties, doubts and fears without any irritable reaching after fact and reason'. It is the recognition that 'our life is of a mingled yarn, good and ill together'. It is the disinterestedness of which Keats spoke as an ideal to be striven for. It is the quality which enabled Shakespeare to look at life through the eyes of a hundred different characters. It is ultimately a form of humility which has as good a claim to be regarded as 'religious' as the 'passionate intensity' of dogmatists.

Whatever Shakespeare's personal views on religion, he could not have given direct expression to them on the Elizabethan or Jacobean stage. But one ought not to exaggerate the secularity of that stage. I agree with those critics who have shown that Elizabethan drama, and Shakespeare's drama in particular, were influenced both by Miracle and Morality plays, and that there is a metaphysical element in nearly all Shakespeare's tragedies. The conflict between passion and reason, between grace and rude will, the belief in sin and damnation, salvation and heaven, are all assumed both by the dramatist and by his audience. In the tragedies set in the Christian era, the heroes all believe that sin carries its punishment. Hamlet fears that the devil has appeared in his father's shape to lure him to damnation; Othello believes that he will suffer everlasting torture for his murder of Desdemona; and Macbeth and his wife ally themselves with the instruments of darkness. Even in the pagan world of *King Lear*, the King, awakening from his madness, imagines that Cordelia is a soul in bliss. Where Shakespeare differs from Calderón is that he avoids all denominational formulations. *Measure for Measure*, we are told, exhibits knowledge of Catholic, Calvinist and Anglican conceptions of Grace; but Shakespeare does not abide our question.

II

Both Calderón and Shakespeare thought of the world as a stage — 'El gran teatro del mundo'. But here again Calderón's treatment of the theme is more specifically religious: men are allotted their parts by God. They are enjoined, though unrehearsed, to do good. The rich man, who is selfish, ends in hell; the peasant, the poor man, and Discretion end in heaven; the still-born child finishes up in limbo. To Shakespeare, in the *Sonnets*, the world was a 'huge stage which presenteth nought but shows', on which the stars comment and which they partially control. To Lear the world was 'this great stage of fools', to Antonio a theatre in which he was given a sad role to

play; to Macbeth, in his despair, life seemed like a bad actor in a
bad melodrama:

> a walking shadow, a poor player
> That struts and frets his hour upon the stage
> And then is heard no more; it is a tale
> Told by an idiot, full of sound and fury,
> Signifying nothing.

In Jaques' speech on the seven ages of man, presumed to be
variations on the motto of the Globe theatre, one man plays
many parts from infancy to senility, not being confined, as in
Calderón, to a single role. But we should not assume that
Shakespeare shared Jaques' cynical views, which are undercut
in this scene by the common humanity of Orlando and the
exiles, as well as by the fact that the seventh age was not
properly one of senility, but as Michael J. B. Allen has pointed
out, the time when one should contemplate the deity and
attain to wisdom.[9] Once again we should beware of assuming
that because Shakespeare is reticent about the divine government of the universe, he rejected belief in it. The influence of
the stars, which he often mentions, is a kind of metaphor for
the influence of Heaven. As Frances Yates pointed out, the
'idea' of the Globe theatre was the theatre of the world; and
that 'to the cosmic meanings of the ancient theatre ... was
added the religious meaning of the theatre as temple, and the
related religious and cosmic meanings of the Renaissance
Church'.[10] Shakespeare's theatre was designed 'to give fullest
support to the voices and the gestures of the players as they
enacted the drama of the life of man within the Theatre of the
World'.

Critics have often called attention to the resemblance between *La vida es sueño* and the speech of Prospero when he
interrupts the nuptial masque. 'Even in dreams', says Clo-
taldo, 'one should not cease from doing good'. Segismundo
replies:

> That's true.
> Then let us check our fury, rage, ambition,
> Lest we should dream again — and dream we will;

For we are in a strange world, where to live
Is but to dream. Experience teaches me
That every man dreams what he is, until
He wakens. One man dreams he is a king,
And in this fond delusion spends his days,
Ruling and monarchizing; but his fame
Is written on the wind. At the touch of death,
Alas, he turns to dust. Can any wish
To reign, when every king must wake at last
In the dream of death? The rich man dreams of wealth,
Which brings him greater care. The poor man dreams
He suffers misery and want. The man
Who starts to prosper, dreams it; who succeeds,
Dreams it; who injures others dreams it too.
And to conclude, although we know it not,
Everyone only dreams the life he leads.
I dream that I am here, weighed down with chains,
But dreamed that I was in a happier state.
What is life? A madness, an illusion,
A shadow, a tale. The greatest good is little.
All life's a dream, and dreams are merely dreams.[11]

(II.ii)

One has to remember the context — that the Prince had been
unjustly imprisoned, released and returned to his prison because he had behaved as a tyrant. So that, whatever Calderón's
beliefs, in the world of the play he is given a second chance,
fortified by his realization that life is illusory. As Vincentio
tells Claudio:

> Thou hast nor youth, nor age,
> But as it were an after-dinner's sleep
> Dreaming on both.
> (*Measure for Measure*, III.i.43-4)

Prospero's speech must also be considered in context. The
masque has been performed by spirits who vanish at his
bidding. He is disturbed by the thought of the conspiracy
against his life, not because he is in any real danger, but because
of his consciousness of the mystery of iniquity. He tells
Ferdinand to be cheerful, since the world itself is as insubstantial as the masque he has just witnessed:

And like the baseless fabric of this vision,
The cloud-capped towers, the gorgeous palaces,
The solemn temples, the great globe itself,
Yea, all which it inherit, shall dissolve,
And like this insubstantial pageant faded
Leave not a rack behind. We are such stuff
As dreams are made on, and our little life
Is rounded with a sleep.

(IV.i.151-8)

The speech links the spirit-actors in the masque with its
audience on the stage (Ferdinand and Miranda) and with the
audience in the theatre. In *The Tempest* Prospero plays the part
of providence, but he is also the protagonist of the action he
has set in motion. So Shakespeare, we may say, creates the
plays in which he himself performs, and the plays are the
medium by which his own experience becomes fully conscious.
The audience identifies with the spectators on the stage, but
they are themselves actors on the stage of the world; and the
dramatist and the actors hold a mirror up to nature, to life
itself, to the divine drama, to what Eliot calls the eternal
action — dreams indeed, but dreams in the mind of God.

III

In a recent article I attempted to show that the writers of love-
comedies are faced with the problem of inventing plausible
postponements of the inevitable happy endings, and I suggested that Calderón and Shakespeare were two of the
dramatists who used the intervening period, between the first
scene and the last, to test the genuineness of the characters'
love.[12] This is apparent in nearly all Shakespeare's comedies,
from *Love's Labour's Lost* to the tragi-comedies of his last
period. Everyone recognizes that Ferdinand and Miranda are
being tested; and when Polixenes threatens Perdita with death
and Florizel with disinheritance, both lovers survive the test.
Florizel proclaims that he is heir to his affection, not to his
father's kingdom:

Not for Bohemia, nor the pomp that may

Be thereat gleaned; for all the sun sees, or
The close earth wombs, or the profound seas hide
In unknown fathoms, will I break my oath
To this my fair beloved.

IV. iv.480-4)

In spite of obvious differences between Calderón's comedies
and Shakespeare's, and between the social customs under
which the two dramatists wrote, in many of Calderón's comedies, too, the lovers are tested. He was aware of the cruelty of
the prevailing code of honour and equally aware of the wrong-
ness of the double standard for men and women. He was
acutely conscious of the difficulties of women in a male-
dominated society. The heroines of several of the comedies use
various stratagems to evade the restrictions imposed on them
so that they can meet the men of their choice. Only by
revolting can the women claim the independence which makes
them something more than sex-objects. The obstacles they
have to overcome include parental disapproval, fraternal con-
ventionality and the jealousy of their possessive lovers. The
men are more conventional, and they do not always rise to the
occasion. Angela, the gay and open-hearted heroine of *La
dama duende*, actually proposes to Don Manuel:

It was for love of you that I became
A phantom in my house; to honour you
Became the living tomb of my own secret.
Indeed, I could not tell you that I loved you,
How much I honoured you; for such an avowal
Would jeopardize your presence as our guest
And make you quit the house. I sought your favour
Because I loved you and I feared to lose you,
Because I wished to cherish and obey you
For term of life, and wed my soul with yours.

(III. iv)

Manuel does not greet this proposal with any enthusiasm. He
dithers, and though he finally agrees to marry the girl, the
audience is bound to feel that she has obtained a poor bargain.

Several of the heroines are suspected on circumstantial
evidence of being unfaithful. In these cases the men are tested

by their treatment of the women they believe to be guilty, the
women by their patience in adversity. In the end, of course, the
heroines are exonerated. But the most interesting play from
this point of view is *Mañanas de abril y mayo* in which Ana is
not explicitly cleared. In Act 2 she tells Juan that if he really
loved her, he would believe in her innocence:

> I would to God my truthful explanation
> About that night could be convincing to you.
> But if it cannot, there's a surer way:
> Reminding you that I am who I am.
> *Juan.*   If only that sufficed!
> *Ana.*   It would do so
>   If you loved me truly.

Juan subsequently discovers that he has unjustly accused her of
making an assignation with another man; and he tacitly admits
that he has been wrong in the other case. He can prove his love
only by trusting Ana: a proof of her innocence would not serve
the same purpose. Ana is implicitly rejecting the right assumed
by all gallants of Golden Age drama to be suspicious of the
conduct of the ladies they profess to love. Such suspicion is an
inevitable result of the way in which women are both idealized
and enslaved, and in which men are predators, jailors and
idolators.

The other heroine of the play, Clara, is more eloquently
rebellious. She is betrothed to a man who expects obedience
from her at the same time as he pursues other women. Liber-
tines violate the nobleman's code of manners as well as
Calderón's code as a Christian. This is why Clara refuses to
marry Hipolito and what gives an edge to her denunciation of
him at the end of Act 2.

> I thought it was small matter for acclaim
> That one mere male should lord it over us;
> And so I sought an opportunity
> To snatch some laurels from him ...
>   You imagined — vain
> And foolish as you are — that in a trice
> You had transfixed the hearts of all the beauties

Parading in the park. Not so, Sir Flirt!
Now learn your lesson; recognise the fact
That your behaviour gives a bad impression
Of love which you profess. This healthy lesson
Leaves Phyllis now avenged for Fabio's scorn.

IV

It is sometimes said that comedies are apt to date more rapidly
than tragedies, if only because they depend more on contemporary customs and ideas; that whereas *Hamlet* and *King
Lear* still speak directly to our hearts and minds, many of
Shakespeare's comedies do not. This is not always true; and
with Calderón the reverse is surely true. We can easily accept
the conventions of society in which the comedies operate, but
with some of the tragedies, because of the differences of
manners and morals, and especially because of the Spanish
conception of honour, the reader or spectator has to overcome
an initial repugnance. It is doubtless according to the custom
of the age — and of some later ages — that the sympathetic
Mayor of Zalamea should try to make an honest woman of his
daughter by marrying her to her rapist; but today the episode
jars.

Then there are a number of plays in which a man murders his
innocent wife on the mere suspicion that she has been unfaithful. The most horrible of these is *El medico de su honra* in
which a man employs a surgeon to bleed his wife to death. The
action is doubtless condemned by the dramatist; but the King,
knowing of the murder, forces the murderer to marry another
woman, who gladly consents.

> *King.*   Give your hand
> To Leonor. It's time for you to repair
> The injuries you've done her.

Guiterre tries to avoid the marriage by confessing to the
murder he has committed; but the King insists:

> *King.* I say that you should clean your door, which bears

The imprint of a bloody hand.
Guit.   But Sire,
Those who exercise a public office
Customarily place upon their door
A shield that bears their arms. My office, Sire,
Is Honour, so I put above my door
My blood-stained hand, since Honour can be washed
With blood alone.
King.   So give your hand to Leonor.
I know she's worthy of it.
Guit.   I obey.
But, Leonor, consider carefully:
It's stained with blood.
Leon.   That does not matter.
I'm not surprised, and I am not afraid.
Guit. Consider, Leonor, that I have been
The doctor of my Honour, and that I
Have not forgot my craft.
Leon.   By means of it
You'll heal my life if it becomes unhealthy.
Guit. On that condition, there's my hand.

                                      (III. vi)

Sometimes, indeed, a husband curses the laws of honour and whoever formulated them:

He little knew the essence of the thing
On which he made the laws.

The theory puts a man's honour in the power of his wife, it takes away his freedom, it makes him the victim of insults and finally makes him answer for a crime against himself. When this husband in *El pintor de su deshonra* has murdered his wife and the man who had kidnapped her, he hopes and expects that the fathers of his victims will avenge themselves on him:

I am a gentleman;
Not cruel; and I seemed to have due cause
To do this bloody honourable deed;
Which done, I will be answerable here
And elsewhere to you all.

                                      (V.v)

The other characters do not condemn him, and he goes free. His apologia resembles the bitter irony of Othello's statement that he may be called 'an honourable murderer', and the words of his final speech:

> Then must you speak
> Of one who loved not wisely but too well;
> Of one not easily jealous, but being wrought
> Perplexed in the extreme; of one whose hand,
> Like the base Indian threw a pearl away
> Richer than all his tribe; of one whose subdu'd eyes,
> Albeit unused to the melting mood,
> Drops tears as fast as the Arabian trees
> Their med'cinable gum.
>
> (V.ii.346-54)

Unlike Othello, Calderón's hero does not kill himself, though it could be argued that to go on living is more of a punishment. In *A secreto agravio, secreta venganza* another husband murders his wife and her supposed lover. The deed must be done secretly, not because he fears retribution, but because open vengeance would reveal that his honour, which depended on his wife's reputation, had been tarnished. It may be mentioned that in the tale which provided Shakespeare with the plot of *Othello*, the Moor and his officer conceal the murder of Desdemona by making the roof fall on her corpse. It is the refusal of Othello to take such precautions, which protects his status as a tragic hero.

Edward M. Wilson suggested that Shakespeare came nearest to Calderonian tragedy in *Othello*, which is essentially a tragedy of honour:[13] of paternal honour in Brabantio, who is disgraced by his daughter's elopement, of professional honour in Cassio, who is sacked for being drunk on duty, and of marital honour in Othello himself. Shakespeare makes it clear that the Moor never ceases to love his wife, and as soon as he finds out that she was innocent, he executes justice on himself, believing that he will be eternally damned. It may not be accidental that his villain is given an apparently Spanish name.

NOTES

1. P. B. Shelley, *The Defence of Poetry* in *Shelley's Literary and Philosophical Criticism*, ed. J. Shawcross (Oxford, 1909), p. 134.

2. A. A. Parker, 'Henry VIII in Shakespeare and Calderón' in *Critical Studies of Calderón's Comedias*, ed. J. E. Varey (Greg International, Farnborough, 1973), pp. 47-83.

3. Edward M. Wilson and Duncan Moir, *A Literary History of Spain: The Golden Age* (Ernest Benn: London, 1971).

4. John Loftis, '*Henry VIII* and Calderón's *La cisma de Inglaterra*', *Comparative Literature*, XXXIV (1982), pp. 208-22.

5. Many critics now believe that Shakespeare wrote the whole play.

6. Assuming that the play was written in 1626-7.

7. Parker, *op. cit.*

8. *Ibid.*

9. Michael J. B. Allen in *Modern Language Quarterly*, XLII (1981), pp. 331-46.

10. Frances Yates, *Theatre of the World* (Routledge: London, 1969), p. 189.

11. This version is partly based on the prose translation by Edward and Elizabeth Huberman. There is a verse translation in Edward Williams' handwriting, but almost certainly by Shelley. It is not surprising that Shelley was attracted to this speech since it chimes with some of his favourite ideas.

12. 'Comedy as a test of Love' in the Eugene Waith *festschrift*, in the press.

13. Published originally in *The Listener* and reprinted in *Spanish and English Literature of the Sixteenth and Seventeenth Centuries* (1980).

9

The Role of Livia In
Women Beware Women

Since T. S. Eliot wrote on Middleton, critics have generally concurred with his opinion that *The Changeling*, though a work of collaboration, and despite the admission that 'it is long-winded and tiresome', was his greatest play. Eliot said nothing about the underplot, which everyone agrees is inferior to the Beatrice plot. As a whole, surely, *Women Beware Women* is the better play. Eliot's account of it concentrates on the decline and fall of Bianca, which can be compared with that of Beatrice; but he does not discuss the equally interesting fall of Isabella, and, more oddly, he omits all mention of the central character, Livia.

It is Livia who unites the two main plots, unites them so well that they cannot be discussed apart. It is she who provides the title of the play, for she brings about the ruin of Bianca in one plot and of Isabella in the other. Her motives are comparatively simple in one case and complex in the other. She hopes for advancement from the Duke by putting Bianca in his power. Yet even here there is a suggestion that she enjoys manipulating other people — an enjoyment symbolized by the game of chess — and dragging them down to her level. She conveniently, if honestly, believes that she is doing Bianca a good turn, and that her initial unwillingness to be the Duke's mistress is caused by a foolish scruple that she will soon outgrow.

Her other success is to persuade Isabella to return Hippolito's love by pretending that they are not really related, her mother having been seduced by a Spanish nobleman. Here Livia's motives are disputed, and they are certainly complex and ambivalent. She is corrupt herself and delights in corrupting others. Isabella, like Bianca, is innocent at the beginning of the play. Like Iago, Livia enjoys making other people her puppets. She has a sisterly fondness for her brother and will do anything to promote his 'happiness'; but, beyond all this, she harbours a suppressed incestuous passion for him, a passion which obtains a vicarious satisfaction from his relationship with her niece.[1]

Livia's first reaction to Hippolito's confession is a conventional one. To love one's kindred sexually is 'unkindly', that is, unnatural. Moreover, to love within such a confined circle is wasteful: the world is full of beautiful women, so why choose one's niece?

> So he Heaven's bounty seems to scorn and mock,
> That spares free means, and spends of his own stock.
>   (II.i.15-16)

After this moralizing, Livia suddenly changes course. The reason she gives is her love for her brother:

>   Nay, I love you so,
> That I shall venture much to keep a change from you
> So fearful as this grief will bring upon you —
> 'Faith, it even kills me, when I see you faint
> Under a reprehension
>   (II.i.18-22)

such as the reproof she has given him. But her next words suggest that the very difficulty of obtaining Isabella's conversion is a challenge to her powers of persuasion and to her ingenuity. 'It is apparently impossible', she seems to be thinking, 'and therefore I'll do it':

>   'tis but a hazarding
> Of grace and virtue, and I can bring forth
> As pleasant fruits as sensuality wishes
> In all her teeming longings. This I can do.
>   (II.i.29-32)

She boasts in her next speech:

> Sir, I could give as shrewd a lift to chastity

As any she that wears a tongue in Florence:
Sh'ad need be a good horsewoman and sit fast
Whom my strong argument could not fling at last
                                    (II.i.36-9)

In fact she is exaggerating her powers of persuasion. It is not by argument that she brings about the falls of Isabella and Bianca. Isabella is convinced by a lie; and Bianca is lured into a trap where she can be seduced, or raped, by the Duke.

She does not name the sin she is snaring Isabella to commit: she remarks that to name it would not be 'handsome'; and she sends Hippolito off, promising to 'minister all cordials' to him:

> a strange cure ...
> As e'er was wrought on a disease so mortal
> And near akin to shame.
>   (II.i.50-2)

The arrival of Isabella is announced by a servant who speaks of her significantly, if unrealistically, as the 'virtuous Isabella'; but, just before her entrance, Livia reaffirms in soliloquy her original motive — love for Hippolito. This love is genuine enough. In the second scene of the play she has told him:

> My best and dearest brother, I could dwell here;
> There is not such another seat on earth
> Where all good parts better express themselves.
>   (I.ii.146-8)

But she knows and admits, despite her frequent euphemisms, that what she is doing is evil. In this respect she is more clear-sighted than Middleton's other female sinners:

> Beshrew you, would I loved you not so well!
> I'll go to bed, and leave this deed undone;
> I am the fondest where I once affect,
> The carefull'st of their healths, and of their ease, forsooth,
> That I look still but slenderly to mine own.
> I take a course to pity him so much now,
> That I have none left for modesty and myself.

> This 'tis to grow so liberal — y'have few sisters
> That love their brother's ease 'bove their own honesties:
> But if you question my affections,
> That will be found my fault.
>
> (II.i 63-73)

There is no reason to doubt that she believes what she says. She has grown 'liberal' — tolerant and permissive — by her fondness for her brother. She is willing to sacrifice her moral standards, or at least the taboo against incest, for the sake of doing him a kindness. It is possible to speak of her, as Margot Heinemann does, as 'the good-natured Court procuress'.[2] But her character and motivation are really more complex. In some ways she resembles the Marquise de Merteuil in Laclos's great novel.

Livia's other success, the procuring of Bianca, is more straightforward. Here she has no moral scruples: she believes that to be a Duke's mistress is obviously better than to be the wife of an impoverished factor. Any regrets expressed by the girl, she ascribes to the inexperience of youth:

> Are you so bitter? 'Tis but want of use;
> Her tender modesty is sea-sick a little,
> Being not accustomed to the breaking billow
> Of woman's wavering faith, blown with temptations.
> 'Tis but a qualm of honour, 'twill away;
> A little bitter for the time, but lasts not.
> Sin tastes at the first draught like wormwood water,
> But drunk again, 'tis nectar ever after.
>
> (II.ii.471-8)

Livia's own downfall, which, with uncharacteristic blindness, she ascribes to ambition — 'My own ambition pulls me down to ruin' — is due rather to her purchase of Leantio's favours and the violence of her attachment to him, which makes her the enemy of the brother she has loved. When Hippolito tries to explain that he killed Leantio to avenge their family honour, Livia cries out the truth of his relations with Isabella:

> The reason! that's a jest hell falls a-laughing at!
> Is there a reason found for the destruction

> Of our more lawful loves? and was there none
> To kill the black lust 'twixt thy niece and thee
> That has kept close so long?
>
> (IV.ii.63-7)

This revelation is the charge which explodes in the last act, for it causes a whole chain of hatreds. Livia hates Hippolito for killing her lover; Hippolito hates Livia for revealing his incestuous relationship; Isabella hates Livia for causing her to commit incest; Guardiano and his Ward hate both Isabella and Hippolito. The reciprocal hatreds make them plot to destroy each other in the masque designed to celebrate the Duke's wedding. Some of the deaths are accidental. Guardiano falls into the trap he had prepared for Hippolito, and the Duke is poisoned by the cup intended for the Cardinal, his brother. But such accidents convey a sense of providential justice more effectively than deliberate killings:

> as if the plagues of sin
> Had been agreed to meet here altogether.
>
> (V.ii.156-7)

We need not greatly concern ourselves with the details of the masque. We know that Livia and Guardiano are plotting against Isabella and Hippolito for making the Ward a cuckold. Isabella is plotting against Livia. In the scene of feigned reconciliation in which they all agree to take part in the masque, Livia is to play her old part of Juno, the goddess of marriage; Isabella is to play the Nymph who offers sacrifice to appease her wrath. This does not quite fit the plot of the masque, in which Juno is not wrathful; but it applies, of course, to Livia's wrath and the sacrifice of Isabella she is planning. Livia remarks:

> Methinks 'twould show the more state in her deity
> To be incensed.
>
> (IV.ii.219-20)

By a nice quibble this looks forward to her death by the poisoned incense, and Isabella has an aside in which she proposes to 'teach a sinful bawd to play a goddess' (IV.ii.221).

The poisoned incense could symbolize the corrupted atmosphere of treachery and lust which emanates from Livia; the shower of fire with which Livia kills Isabella could likewise symbolize the unwitting incest, and the witting adultery, committed by the victim. Juno in her first lines says that the affections of the three suitors:

> Seem all as dark to our illustrious brightness
> As night's inheritance, hell ...
>
> (V.ii.103-4)

The cupids — Livia's pages — shoot Hippolito with their poisoned arrows, symbolizing his incestuous love. Guardiano, the pander, falls into the trap prepared for Hippolito, the accident presumably being due to his foolish ward.

It is given to Hippolito to point the moral:

> Lust and forgetfulness has been amongst us,
> And we are brought to nothing.
> ·
> Leantio's death
> Has brought all this upon us — now I taste it —
> And made us lay plots to confound each other:
> The event so proves it; and man's understanding
> Is riper at his fall than all his lifetime.
> She, in a madness for her lover's death,
> Revealed a fearful lust in our near bloods,
> For which I am punished dreadfully and unlooked for;
> Proved her own ruin too: vengeance met vengeance
> Like a set match.
> ·
> But how her fawning partner fell, I reach not,
> Unless caught by some springe of his own setting —
> For on my pain, he never dreamed of dying;
> The plot was all his own, and he had cunning
> Enough to save himself: but 'tis the property
> Of guilty deeds to draw your wise men downward.
> Therefore the wonder ceases.
>
> (V.ii.144-64)

Not every member of the audience is likely to follow every

detail of this last scene, but everyone will obtain a general impression of what is happening. If one listens to the words one is told plainly that Isabella, as she confesses, has poisoned Livia; Isabella's death is explained by Hippolito; Hippolito knows he has been wounded by poisoned arrows; and Bianca confesses that the Duke has drunk the poison intended for the Cardinal. At the last production at Stratford-upon-Avon, however, the action was not made clear, largely because the director was anxious to draw a thematic parallel between the chess game of Act 2 and the masque of Act 5.[3]

G.R. Hibbard has severely criticized Middleton for the way he kills off all his main characters without bothering about motivation,[4] and other critics have regarded Hippolito's sudden concern for family honour a mere theatrical device to precipitate the final catastrophe. This concern surprises, but it is not implausible. A more serious flaw is the motivation of the Cardinal, the spokesman for morality in the second half of the play. In the first scene of Act 4 he warns the Duke that he will certainly be damned if he continues to keep a mistress:

> and fall into
> A torment that knows neither end nor bottom
> For beauty but the deepness of a skin ...
> (IV.i.243–5)

The Duke, who has just incited Hippolito to kill Leantio, professes to be repentant, and swears that he will never more keep a woman unlawfully. The Cardinal is delighted, not knowing that the Duke was proposing to have Leantio murdered so that he could marry Bianca. On his next appearance, the Cardinal tries to prevent the marriage because it was being used as a cloak for lust — 'lust's offerings ... on wedlock's sacred altar'. The Duke protests that he has kept to the letter of his vow, and Bianca complains of the Cardinal's lack of charity. Middleton, I believe, was never the detached observer of Eliot's imagination, and a spokesman for orthodox morality is desirable at this point in the play. What is less satisfactory is that Middleton makes no attempt to explain how the Cardinal has become reconciled to the marriage he has passionately denounced; and he gives only a perfunctory explanation of Bianca's motives in attempting to murder him. But the car-

dinal's presence in the last scene enables Middleton to dispose
of the two principal sinners not involved in the masque; and, as
the only important surviving character — and as almost the
only virtuous cardinal in the whole of Jacobean drama — the
Cardinal can pronounce with the authority of the Church the
final judgement on the characters of the play and on the
destruction which has overtaken them:

> Sin, what thou art, these ruins show too piteously!
> Two kings on one throne cannot sit together
> But one must needs down, for his title's wrong:
> So where lust reigns, that prince cannot reign long.
> (V.ii.220–3)

Livia is dangerous to other women for the reasons we have
outlined. She is clear-sighted, she knows what she wants, and
she is without scruples. Above all, she is a good psychologist
and knows how to turn the weaknesses of others to good
account. But it is important to recognize that her two chief
victims, although they come to commit adultery and murder,
are initially innocent. They are not, like Beatrice, moral
morons.

Bianca, who elopes with Leantio, is prepared to accept a
much lower standard of living than the one to which she is
accustomed. She marries for love; and, if some difficulties of
adjustment may be expected, her love is genuine and involves
sacrifice of worldly standards. As she is almost as young as
Juliet, she can hardly be expected to realize the defects of
character hidden beneath Leantio's handsome exterior. However much Leantio is enamoured of his wife's beauty, there is
something egotistical and possessive about his love. The
language he uses about her is all in terms of treasure that he
owns.[5] She is an invaluable purchase, a treasure, a beauty able
to content a conqueror, a noble theft; her beauty is her dowry,
her virtues are jewels locked up in cabinets. He urges his
mother not to teach her to rebel by suggesting that he is unable
to support her in the way to which she is accustomed. It would,
of course, be wrong to suggest that his love is not genuine, but
the imagery implies that he regards her as a possession which
he is proud of acquiring. Moreover, it suits his commercial

occupation. Bianca's own expression of love is less open to criticism. She tells her mother-in-law:

> Kind mother, there is nothing can be wanting
> To her that does enjoy all her desires.
> Heaven send a quiet peace with this man's love,
> And I am as rich, as virtue can be poor ...
>
>   (I.i.125–8)

At the end of the scene Leantio decides to ask his mother to ensure that his jewel is not seen by others when he is away on business:

>   O fair-eyed Florence!
> Didst thou but know what a most matchless jewel
> Thou now art mistress of —
> ....
>   But 'tis great policy
> To keep choice treasures in obscurest places:
> Should we show thieves our wealth, 'twould make 'em
>   bolder.
> ....
> The jewel is cased up from all men's eyes:
> Who could imagine now a gem were kept,
> Of that great value, under this plain roof?
>
>   (I.i.161–72)

In the next scene in which Leantio appears, he is torn between feelings of uxoriousness and his business. Game in a new-married couple, he says, spoils all thrift. Bianca begs him to stay for one more night, and he reads her a lesson:

>   love that's wanton must be ruled awhile
> By that that's careful, or all goes to ruin.
> As fitting is a government in love
> As in a kingdom; where 'tis all mere lust
> 'Tis like an insurrection in the people
> That, raised in self-will, wars against all reason:
> But love that is respective for increase
> Is like a good king, that keeps all in peace.
>
>   (I.iii.41–8)

We can see here the beginnings of a clash between bourgeois principles and the claims of love.

When the Duke's messenger arrives, Bianca is commanded to hide: she is 'a gem no stranger's eye must see'; but when she insists on going to the banquet, Leantio declares that wedlock is 'the ripe time of man's misery' and he applies the jewel imagery to celibacy:

>   What a peace
> Has he that never marries! if he knew
> The benefit he enjoyed, or had the fortune
> To come and speak with me, he should know then
> The infinite wealth he had, and discern rightly
> The greatness of his treasure by my loss. (III.i.280–5)

At the banquet he speaks of himself as 'the poor thief that stole the treasure', and he imagines he is being punished for the pain he has caused Bianca's relatives. He is very conscious of the fact that he is her social inferior.

The chess scene is one of Middleton's greatest triumphs, not least because the class difference between Livia and Leantio's mother is brilliantly suggested. They are neighbours, and the old woman is invited, out of charity, to Sunday dinner and Thursday supper. Lamb regarded the scene as a faithful transcript from life. Livia, he said, 'is as real a creature as one of Chaucer's characters. She is such another jolly housewife as the Wife of Bath.' This remark shows how 'specimens' can be misleading. Livia is pretending to be more neighbourly than she really is, and, unlike the Wife of Bath, she is a wealthy aristocrat. The class difference between the two women is brought out by the deference paid by the mother to her hostess. Bianca, after her seduction by the Duke, contrasts the poverty of Leantio's home with the standard of living she had formerly enjoyed: she regards as necessities what her mother-in-law regards as unobtainable luxuries. Later in the play the Duke knows that Hippolito will be horrified at the news that Livia is having an affair with a mere factor; and Leantio behaves with vulgar ostentation as a middle-aged woman's gigolo.

Bianca is trapped by Livia and Guardiano, and she puts up

more than a token resistance to the Duke. We should remember that she still loves her husband at this point in the play, and her first exclamation when she encounters the Duke is: 'Oh treachery to honour!' (II.ii.321). She struggles in his grasp, and her struggles merely increase his lust. She tells him that if adultery is not a sin, 'there's no religion' (line 349). She calls 'for strength to virtue' (line 359). The Duke makes it clear that, whatever she does, she is not going to escape him. He prefers 'A passionate pleading 'bove an easy yielding' (line 361). But he warns her that he:

> never pitied any: they deserve none
> That will not pity me. I can command:
> Think upon that.
>
> (II.ii.362–4)

He speaks, finally, of the advantages of being loved by him: freedom from poverty, vain regrets that she has married a man who cannot give her the luxuries her beauty deserves and 'glory', which he urges her to seize. Bianca doesn't reply and we can assume that she has been cowed into submission more than tempted by what the Duke offers. After her seduction she curses the two who engineered it. Guardiano congratulates himself on his achievement:

> Never were finer snares for women's honesties
> Than are devised in these days ...
>
> (II.ii.398–9)

but Bianca tells him:

> sin and I'm acquainted,
> No couple greater; and I'm like that great one
> Who, making politic use of a base villain,
> 'He likes the treason well, but hates the traitor';
> So I hate thee, slave.
>
> (II.ii.441–5)

Her quotation from Machiavelli reveals her ambivalent attitude to her adultery, and it is a prelude to her moral deterioration in the rest of the play. But Eliot, I believe, is wrong to state that her fall is due to vanity. It is due rather to the temptation of wealth, made the more powerful by the contrast between the life-style of her family and that of Leantio, and also to a realization that her adultery, however unwilling, cannot be undone.

The deterioration is apparent already in Act 3. Her continual complaints to her mother-in-law contrast with her contentedness in the first scene of the play; her refusal of a kiss from Leantio contrasts with her former demand for kisses; and the apparent absence of moral qualms in her insistence on going to the banquet are indications that she hopes now for the things the Duke has promised her. In the banquet scene, she makes disparaging remarks about marriage and cuckolds, knowing that Leantio will overhear. In Act 4 she and Leantio have a sordid slanging-match, and immediately afterwards she acquiesces in his murder. She cannot forgive the Cardinal's condemnation of her adultery and plots to have him poisoned. The innocent girl has developed into a ruthless killer.

She does not entirely forfeit the sympathy of the audience. Her relationship with the Duke after her unwilling seduction, has changed from acquiescence to ambition, and as the final scene shows, to love. She is given no conventional speeches of repentance, although she feels she is being justly punished for her adultery. She kisses the lips of the dead Duke in the hope of absorbing some of the poison. Some of it, indeed, burns her lips and face, and, as she says 'A blemished face best fits a leprous soul' (V.ii.203). This line, as Roma Gill suggests, reminds the audience of Bianca's first reactions after her seduction:[6]

> Yet since mine honour's leprous, why should I
> Preserve that fair that caused the leprosy?
> Come, poison all at once!
>
> (II.ii.425-7)

As she dies, she is completely isolated; the mistress, even the wife, of a dead duke, who is a self-confessed murderess, has no tolerable future:

> What make I here? these are all strangers to me,

Not known but by their malice, now th'art gone,
Nor do I seek their pities.

(V.ii.204-6)

Middleton makes her remind us that the original fall was
involuntary, and remind us too of the title of the play:

Oh the deadly snares
That women set for women — without pity
Either to soul or honour! Learn by me
To know your foes. In this belief I die:
Like our own sex, we have no enemy.

(V.ii.209-13)

She tastes the same death as the Duke in a cup of love, and the
hated Cardinal is left to rule Florence.

Livia's other victim, Isabella, is depicted with still more
initial sympathy. She has been created merely to be 'a saleable
product'.[7] She is about to be married, against her wishes, to the
Ward. Her father is sacrificing his daughter's happiness for
sordid mercenary reasons, so that Livia is moved to protest:

I ... call't injustice
To force her love to one she never saw.
Maids should both see and like ...

(I.ii.30-2)

The ward, moreover, is half-witted, coarse and vulgar, and
Middleton plainly agrees with Isabella's plaint:

Marry a fool!
Can there be greater misery to a woman
That means to keep her days true to her husband,
And know no other man, so virtue wills it!
Why, how can I obey and honour him,
But I must needs commit idolatry?
A fool is but the image of a man,
And that but ill made neither.

(I.ii.161-8)

Contrasted with this obvious misalliance is the marriage of
true minds exemplified in the close friendship of Isabella and

Hippolito. This is vouched for by Isabella's father and the Ward's uncle:

> Those two are nev'r asunder; they've been heard
> In argument at midnight, moonshine nights
> Are noondays with them; they walk out their sleeps —
> Or rather at those hours appear like those
> That walk in 'em ...
>
> (I.ii.63–7)

When they approach, Guardiano, the disreputable pander, exclaims:

> Oh affinity,
> What piece of excellent workmanship art thou?
> 'Tis work clean wrought, for there's no lust, but love in't,
> And that abundantly ...
>
> (I.ii.69–72)

Of course, the lines prove to be ironical, although Isabella is not aware of the sexual element in her friendship with her uncle.

When Hippolito involuntarily confesses his love, Isabella is at first too innocent to understand his meaning, and when she does understand, she is horrified:

> Farewell all friendly solaces and discourses;
> I'll learn to live without ye, for your dangers
> Are greater than your comforts. What's become
> Of truth in love, if such we cannot trust.
> When blood that should be love is mixed with lust!
>
> (I.ii.225–9)

When Livia purports to prove that she is not related to Hippolito, Isabella immediately proposes to take him as a lover and to conceal their relationship by marrying the Ward. This is the beginning of her moral deterioration, although Holmes is surely wrong to suggest that 'The word "love" is used mockingly throughout the play', that Hippolito is satirized, and that Isabella has only been posing as a platonic lover.[8] When Livia reveals the truth, Isabella's farewell to

Hippolito reveals not merely how far she has been corrupted
but also the distinction she makes between the shame and
horror of incest and what she still feels is a comparatively
innocent adultery:

> 'Tis time we parted, sir, and left the sight
> Of one another; nothing can be worse
> To hurt repentance — for our very eyes
> Are far more poisonous to religion
> Than basilisks to them. If any goodness
> Rest in you, hope of comforts, fear of judgements,
> My request is, I nev'r may see you more;
> And so I turn me from you everlastingly,
> So is my hope to miss you.
>   (IV.ii.133–41)

As Eliot says, 'in flashes and when the dramatic need comes',
Middleton is 'a great poet, a great master of versifiction'.

In a less corrupt society, and in one less dominated by greed,
both Bianca and Isabella might have led happy and virtuous
lives; and one cannot say of them, as Eliot said of Beatrice, that
they 'become moral only by becoming damned'. Although
they both become involved in mortal sin through 'the stamp of
one defect', the instrument of their ruin is Livia. Middleton
intends us to pity them.

NOTES

1. The point is made by Roma Gill, among others, in her New
   Mermaids' edition (1968), xxiii. Later citation is from this
   edition.
2. Margot Heinemann, *Puritanism and Theatre* (Cambridge,
   1980), p. 183.
3. The best account of the masque is in Inga-Stina Ewbank's
   essay, '"These pretty devices": a Study of Masques in Plays',
   A Book of Masques (Cambridge, 1967), pp. 405–48.
4. G.R. Hibbard, 'The Tragedies of Thomas Middleton and the
   Decadence of the Drama', *Renaissance and Modern Studies*,
   I (1957) 35–64. Hibbard argues that Middleton was inhibited by

three things: the idea that a tragedy should end in a blood-bath, that it should be overtly moral and that it should contain comic relief. As a result, the naturalistic, psychological drama of the first three acts turns into a melodramatic revenge play, with Middleton doing violence to his characters; and the overtly religious speeches of the Cardinal are 'alien to the whole tone and significance of the earlier part of the play ... What begins as something that might not be unfittingly described as seventeenth-century Ibsen, ends as a kind of mongrel, the illegitimate offspring of an incongruous union between *The Revenger's Tragedy* and *A Warning for Fair Women*' (pp. 53, 54). I doubt whether the audience's expectations were quite as Hibbard suggests and, in any case, I do not think Middleton was inhibited by them, or that he suffered from a failure of nerve.

5. See C.B. Ricks's article, 'Word-Play in *Women Beware Women*', *Review of English Studies*, N.S. 12 (1961), 238–50.
6. Gill, ed. cit., p. 111.
7. Hibbard, *op. cit.*, p. 46.
8. David M. Holmes, *The Art of Thomas Middleton* (Clarendon Press: Oxford 1970), pp. 165, 166.

10

Two Plays Reconsidered:
More Dissemblers Besides Women and *No Wit, No Help like a Woman's*

Two sides of Middleton's dramatic work have received reasonable recognition, both in the theatre and from the critics. In the last few months [of 1979] there have been at least four productions in England of *The Changeling*, and in the last few years there have been several productions of *Women Beware Women*. The critics have treated the tragedies with enthusiasm or respect. The same thing may be said of the city comedies: *A Chaste Maid in Cheapside* has been revived several times, and the curious playgoer has had the chance to see *A Trick to Catch the Old One* and one or two other comedies. Both kinds of play get reprinted in anthologies of Jacobean drama, in the two-volume selection in the original Mermaid Dramatists, in the New Mermaids and in the Regents series. There have, moreover, been two good books on citizen comedy as a genre.

It is the purpose of this article to suggest that such a concentration on two groups of plays does an injustice to Middleton, whose work is more varied than this. *A Game of Chess*, for example, is a masterpiece in a totally different kind of play. But I want in this article to consider two plays which are, in their different ways, masterly. They are not without flaws, for the 'impure art' of Middleton — as much as that of Webster — causes occasional embarrassment, as all recent productions have shown, even in *The Changeling* and *Women Beware Women*.

The first of the two plays I want to discuss, *More Dissemblers Besides Women*, was in fact published in the same volume as *Women Beware Women*, but it has been treated very perfunctorily by all recent critics. It is a black comedy on the

theme of dissembling — conscious hypocrisy in some characters, self-deception in others. Only General Andrugio is
completely free of it, and even he disguises himself to rescue his
love. The Cardinal continually eulogizes the Duchess for her
refusal to remarry seven years after the death of her first
husband, and he thinks of her as the triumph of his teaching,
a living exemplar of chastity:

> So dear her white fame is to my soul's love
> 'Tis an affliction but to hear it question'd:
> She's my religious triumph,
>
>   (I.ii.62-4)[1]

until he is led to believe that the Duchess has fallen in love with
his nephew, Lactantio. Up to this point, he had praised
Lactantio for his pretended horror at the thought of sex; but
now he urges on the young man, and on the Duchess, their
duty to marry. Middleton satirizes his sudden change of
attitude, and that of the attendant lords who parrot his
opinions:

> How think you now, Lords?
> If she that might offend safe does not err,
> What's chaste in others is most rare in her.
>
> 2 *Lord.*   What wisdom but approves it?
>
> 1 *Lord.*   But my Lord,
> This should be told to her it concerns most;
> Pity such good things should be spoke and lost.
>
> *Card.*   That were the way to lose 'em utterly:
> You quite forget her vow. Yet now I think on't,
> What is that vow? 'Twas but a thing enforc'd,
> Was it not, Lords?
>
> 1 *Lord.*   Merely compelled indeed.
>
> *Card.*   Only to please the Duke; and forc'd virtue
> Fails in her merit — there's no crown prepar'd for it.
> What have we done, my Lords? I fear we have sinn'd
> In too much strictness to uphold her in't.
>
>   (II.i.285-98)

The Cardinal does not mention that the Duchess (as he mistakenly thinks) wants to marry his nephew. But Middleton leaves it open whether the Cardinal is a deliberate or an unconscious hypocrite. His views at the beginning of the play about the desirability of refraining from sex and marriage are presumably genuine, but he is jolted out of them by the prospect of a wealthy alliance.

The Duchess, though depicted with greater sympathy, is another self-deceiver. She had promised her dying husband never to remarry, and she had kept the vow for seven years, living a cloistered life and continually strenthened by the Cardinal's exhortations and flatteries. When she does fall in love with the victorious General Andrugio, she is led into a whole series of deceptions, pretending that she hates him and loves Lactantio; and when she discovers that Andrugio loves another woman, she is outraged by his choice and thinks he must be out of his mind, for Aurelia is disguised as a gipsy. She declares:

> a wrong done to beauty
> Is greater than an injury done to love,
> And we'll less pardon it; for had it been
> A creature whose perfection had out-shin'd me,
> It had been honourable judgement in him,
> And to my peace a noble satisfaction.
>
> (V.ii.60-65)

But when Aurelia comes back, cleaned up and without her disguise, the Duchess has to admit that the Andrugio has made a worthy choice:

> I have no wrong at all; she's younger, fairer;
> He has not now dishonour'd me in choice;
> I much commend his noble care and judgement.
> (V.ii.128-130)

She therefore gives her blessing to the marriage. She decides to retire into 'some religious sanctuary' and give up her wealth to 'holy uses' (V.ii.202,201).

Aurelia, another dissembler, disguises herself as a man to facilitate her love-affair with Lactantio, but when she meets her father, who intends to marry her off to the aged Governor of the Fort, her disguise is at once penetrated. When she is imprisoned, she pretends she is still in love with Andrugio — 'welcome to my lips / As morning dew to roses' (I.iii.37-38) — so that he will help her to escape. She disguises herself as a gipsy and agrees to be Dondolo's doxy and dell. In the final scene, when the Duchess lets her choose a husband — assuming she will choose Andrugio — she turns to Lactantio and says:

> Spread thy arms open wide, to welcome her
> That has wrought all this means to rest in thee.
>
> (V.ii.141-2)

Only when she is scornfully repulsed by Lactantio does she ask, and receive, forgiveness from the long-suffering Andrugio.

The greatest dissembler, however, is Lactantio, who pretends to his uncle he is virginal and celibate, while he has one cast-off mistress who is about to bear his child, and to whom he had promised marriage, and a current mistress. Aurelia, whom he jilts so that he can marry the Duchess. He is sexually promiscuous, but yet contrives to appear to his uncle as a celibate misogynist. His blood appears to be 'very snow-broth', as Shakespeare's Lucio says of Angelo. He never seems to feel the wanton stings and motions of the sense. His secrecy is caused by his desire to inherit from his uncle, and his downfall is caused by ambition — the hope of marrying the Duchess, who is older and less sexually attractive than either of his two mistresses. His hypocrisy is the result of a conflict in his mind between lust and ambition. His callousness is revealed over and over again, by his breaking promises of marriage, as he confesses, to numerous women:

> With strange oaths, quotha!
> They're not so strange to me. I have sworn the same things
> I am sure forty times over...
> . . . .
> If I should marry all those I have promis'd
> 'Twould make one vicar hoarse, ere he could dispatch us.
>
> (III.i.16-18, 21.2)

These remarks are made to his cast-off mistress, now pregnant and disguised as a page. He is even more brutal when he is forced by the Duchess to marry the girl:

> Curse of this fortune! This 'tis to meddle with taking
> stuff, whose belly cannot be confined in a waist-band.
> Pray, what have you done with the breeches! We shall
> have need of 'em shortly: and we get children so fast,
> they are too good to be cast away. My son and heir
> need not scorn to wear what his mother left off. I
> had my fortune told me by a gipsy seven years ago:
> she said that I should be the spoil of many a maid,
> and at seven years' end marry a quean for my labour —
> which falls out wicked and true.
>
> (V.ii.249-58)

The girl has engaged the sympathies of the audience in the pathetically comic scene in which her dancing lesson is interrupted by her cry for a midwife. Middleton makes no pretence that the marriage will be a happy one, any more than Shakespeare pretends that Kate Keepdown will be happy with Lucio.

Lactantio is equally brutal in his dismissal of Aurelia when she claims the fulfillment of his promise to marry her:

> *Lact.* Prithee away, fond fool; hast' no shame in thee?
> Thou'rt bold and ignorant, whate'er thou art.
>
> *Aur.* What e'er I am? Do you not know me then?
>
> *Lact.* Yes, for some waiting-vessel; but the times
> Are chang'd with me. if y'had the grace to know 'em.
> I look'd for more respect. I am not spoke withal
> After this rate, I tell you. Learn hereafter
> To know what belongs to me. You shall see
> All the Court teach you shortly. Farewell, manners.
>
> (V.ii.144-52)

Yet, despite Lactantio's character and behavior, he arouses some admiration for his skill in dissembling — as Richard III, Edmund and even Iago do. There is a nice contrast between the first scene of the play, where we see him dallying with Aurelia, and his appearance in the second scene, where he enters reading a book, and tells the Cardinal:

> I wonder at the young men of our days,
> That they can dote on pleasure, or what 'tis
> They give that title to, unless in mockage;
> There's nothing I can find upon the earth
> Worthy the name of pleasure...
> . . . .
> But of all the frenzies
> That follow flesh and blood, O reverend uncle,
> The most ridiculous is to fawn on women;
> There's no excuse for that; 'tis such a madness,
> There is no cure set down for't.   (I.ii.107-17)

A few moments later, his former mistress, now disguised as a
page tells him she is pregnant. In a later scene, when his uncle
urges him to marry the Duchess, he still pretends to find
women distasteful:

> I know not what love is, or what you speak of:
> If woman be amongst it, I shall swoon;...
> Most serious uncle, name no such thing to me.
>   (III.i.167-70)

Like the heroes of Restoration comedy — Dorimant, Horner
or Valentine — his promiscuity is not regarded as particularly
deplorable. Moreover the Cardinal's views on sex are so
perverted that we can even applaud his nephew's deception of
him. Ever since T.S. Eliot's brilliant, if misleading, essay on
Middleton, many critics have echoed his view that Middleton
'has no message; he is merely a great recorder.'[2] This remark
seems to me to be quite untrue of the author of the great
tragedies, if it means that he has no moral standpoint. It is
more nearly true of *More Dissemblers*, though even here there
is no doubt where he stands in his exposure of hypocrisy and
self-deception, and in the sympathy he arouses for forsaken
women.

The theatrical brilliance of the play can be illustrated by an
examination of the final scene in which there are a dozen
surprises and rehearsals. First, the Duchess proposes to dis-
miss Celia for declaring that Andrugio is in love with a gipsy;
and when she sees Aurelia in disguise, she supposes that
Andrugio has gone mad. When Andrugio comes in, it is

obvious that he is perfectly sane, and he denies that he loves a gipsy. Next Aurelia is brought in undisguised, and the Duchess generously admits that she is fairer and younger than herself. She approves of the marriage; but to the astonishment of both the Duchess and Andrugio, Aurelia lays claim to Lactantio. To Aurelia's astonishment, Lactantio repudiates her, so she falls back on her first love, Andrugio. The Cardinal asks the Duchess to choose a husband from the assembled lords, and Lactantio is confident that he will be chosen. To everyone's surprise — and to the chagrin of the Cardinal and Lactantio — the Duchess decides to become a nun. Lactantio realizes that he has lost both the Duchess and Aurelia through his ambition:

> This is to hawk at eagles. Pox of pride!
> It lays a man i'th 'mire still, like a jade
> That has too many tricks, and ne'er a good one.
> I must gape high; I'm in a sweet case now;
> I was sure of one, and now I have lost her too.
>
> (V.ii.205-9)

The Duchess then reveals that her 'Page' has been made pregnant by Lactantio 'near forty weeks ago' (V.ii.215). Lactantio admits, aside, 'I'm paid with mine own money' (V.ii.225). The Cardinal, outraged at his hypocrisy, disowns him:

> I utterly disclaim all blood in thee,
> I'll sooner make a parricide my heir
> Than such a monster. (V.ii.226-8)

Finally the Duchess demands that the Cardinal should forgive him, since he had had 'punishment enough in his false hopes' (V.ii.240-241). Moreover, she gives ten thousand ducats to the 'page' as a dowry. She concludes by saying:

> We all have faults: look not so much on his.
> Who lives i'th world that never did amiss?
> . . . .
> Oh, they that search out man's intents shall find
> There's more dissemblers than of womankind.
>
> (V.ii.259-60, 267-8)

The play, as we have suggested, is not without weaknesses, some of which could be cut in performance. Dondolo, like most of Middleton's comic servants, is not very funny; and the scene with the gipsies, attractive as it may have been to Jacobean audiences, is somewhat tedious to us. But, despite these flaws, the general design of the play, and its portraits of dissembling, are masterly.

The other play, *No Wit, No Help Like a Woman's,* has had few admirers. Swinburne, indeed, spoke of the energetic invention and 'the unfailing charm of a style worthy of Fletcher himself', but now Fletcher's reputation is so much lower than it was in the nineteenth century, when he was rated second only to Shakespeare, Middleton appears to be damned with faint praise.[3] The play was summarily dismissed by Barker and Holmes, and not mentioned by Dorothy Farr.[4] It deserves more attention.

It contains two well-integrated plots, in both of which there is a happy ending through the intervention of women — the 'wit' of Kate, and the 'help' of Lady Twilight. Kate's husband, Low-water, has been brought to penury through the sharp practice of Goldenfleece, recently deceased. Low-water is apathetic and without hope, so Kate takes matters into her own hands. Her opportunity cames when Sir Gilbert Lampton, a suitor for Lady Goldenfleece's hand, writes Kate a letter, proposing to set her up as his mistress with the money he will obtain from the wealthy marriage. Kate then disguises herself as a gallant, with her husband acting as her servant, and joins Lady Goldenfleece's band of suitors. By revealing Sir Gilbert's perfidy she is able to steal a march on the other suitors, and she is chosen by the grateful widow. On the wedding night, by means of a trick, she catches her bride in a compromising situation, compelling the restoration of the money of which her husband had been cheated. Only then does she reveal her sex.

The other plot is even more complex. It is based on a play entitled *La Sorella* by Giambattista Della Porta.[6] This is very close to Middleton's underplot, as a summary will make clear. Attilio is sent to ransom his mother and sister from the Turks, but he does not get further than Venice where he falls in love with Sofia, a slave-girl, and spends the ransom money on her.

He reports the death of his mother and claims that Sofia is his sister. His father proposes to marry Sofia to the Captain, and Attilio to Sulpizia, whom his best friend loves. At this point, as with Middleton, the play begins. In Act 3 a friend arrives from Constantinople with the news that Attilio's mother is alive, and he recognizes Sofia as the slave-girl. The comic servant pretends to talk Turkish with the friend's son. When the mother arrives, she at once agrees to forgive Attilio and to pretend that Sofia is her daughter. When she meets the girl, she is convinced that she really is. Attilio laments his unwitting incest at some length; but all ends happily because it turns out that Sofia and Sulpizia had been exchanged in infancy by a nurse who wanted her own child to have the benefits of a wealthy home. This full-length play is the basis of only a third of Middleton's and our attitude to it is altered by the juxta-position of the Low-water plot.

Middleton's alterations, apart from questions of tone, are straightforward. He substitutes pirates for Turks, Antwerp for Venice, a Dutch merchant for the friend from Constan-tinople, Weatherwise for the Captain; and he leaves Grace's occupation vague. Otherwise, Middleton follows Della Porta closely. Before the play opens, Philip Twilight has been sent by his father with the ransom to procure the release of his wife, captured by pirates and imprisoned for nine years, and also their daughter, Philip's sister. But Philip had squandered the money, had fallen in love with a girl he had come across in an inn at Antwerp, married her and brought her back to England as his long-lost sister. (We are not told what the girl was doing alone in the inn, but we are bound to suspect her profession). Philip reported that his mother was dead. All goes well until Sir Oliver proposes to marry his 'daughter' to Weatherwise and to marry Philip to Jane Sunset, who is loved by Sandfield, Philip's closest friend. The friends quarrel because Sandfield thinks that Philip has intrigued so that he can marry Jane.

This is the situation at the beginning of the play, and it is brilliantly conveyed to the audience by means of the quarrel and the resulting explanations. Savorwit, the cunning servant, has an ingeious solution to the problem. He will tell Sir Oliver that Sandfield is in love with his daughter and will take her without a dowry. As Sir Oliver strongly objects to the pro-

vision of dowries, this will dispose of Weatherwise. Philip and
Sandfield will then go through a form of marriage with the
wrong girls; but as they will all be living under Sir Oliver's
roof, they can exchange wives at night:

> In the daytime,
> To please the old man's eyesight, you may dally,
> And set a kiss on the wrong lip — no sin in't,
> Brothers and sisters do't, cousins do more;
> But, pray, take heed you be not kin to them:
> So in the night-time nothing can deceive you,
> Let each know his own work.
>   (I.i.137-43)

It is an ingenious scheme. Sir Oliver gets rid of Weatherwise
and accepts Sandfield as a suitor to his daughter. But before
the end of the first act the whole scheme is threatened by the
arrival of a Dutch merchant with a message for Sir Oliver from
his wife (who is not dead as Philip had reported) and he
recognizes Grace as a girl he had seen in an inn at Antwerp.
Savorwit tries to brazen it out, but Philip is driven to despera-
tion. The actual speech is revealing. He is appalled much more
by the loss of his wife than by the revelation of his treachery to
his mother.

> 'Tis not the bare news of my mother's life —
> May she live long and happy! — that afflicts me.
> With half the violence that the latter draws;
> Though in that news I have my share of grief;
> As I had share of sin and a foul neglect;
> It is my love's betraying, that's the sting
> That strikes through flesh and spirit.
>   (II.ii.12-18)

This is the reason why he tries to kill himself.

When Philip's mother arrives, Savorwit advises him to
confess and throw himself on her mercy. This episode is one
that readers find difficult to accept because of the unbelievably
forgiving attitude of Lady Twilight, and because they know
that Philip is confessing out of policy. He had spent her
ransom and reported that she was dead, but she seems to
regard it as merely a minor peccadillo.

Phil.   Provide forgiveness then, for that's the want
My conscience feels. Oh, my wild youth has led me
Into unnatural wrongs against your freedom once:
I spent the ransom which my father sent
To set my pleasures free, while you lay captive,
. . . .
Lady Twi.   And is this all now?
You use me like a stranger; pray stand up.
Phil.   Rather fall flat; I shall deserve yet worse
Lady Twi.   (*raising him*) Whate'er your faults, esteem me
                            still a friend
Or else you wrong me more in asking pardon
Than when you did the wrong you ask'd it for;
And since you have prepar'd me to forgive you,
Pray let know for what: the first fault's nothing.
. . . .
Phil.   Here comes the wrong then that drives home the rest.
I saw a face at Antwerp, that quite drew me
From conscience and obedience; in that fray
I lost my heart, I must needs lose my way.
There went the ransom, to redeem my mind;
Stead of the money, I brought over her,
And to cast mists before my father's eyes
Told him it was my sister, lost so long,
And that yourself was dead — you see the wrong
. . . .
But such is the hard plight my state lives in,
That 'twixt forgiveness, I must sin again
And seek my help where I bestow'd my wrongs.
Oh mother! pity once, though against reason!
                            (II.ii.116-38, 145-48)

He asks her to say that the girl was indeed his sister. Lady
Twilight, from maternal devotion rather than Christian forgiveness, agrees to his request, deceiving her husband in the
process.

Philip thinks that he is out of the wood; but to his horror,
Lady Twilight, on questioning the girl, is convinced that she
really is his sister. The relationship has been incestuous.

I have suggested that the way we react to the Della Porta
story is affected by its subordinate position in Middleton's
play and by the contrast between it and the main plot. In the

first place, the virtuous Kate — an almost Shakespearian heroine transported from the world of Arden or Illyria to the corrupt realities of Jacobean London — must leave the audience with very little sympathy for the anti-hero, Philip. The heroes of all the citizen comedies are unscrupulous, but none is quite as callous as Philip is in leaving his mother in captivity. Moreover, those heroes outwit the old and the avaricious, who are no better morally than themselves. Of course, even Kate is tough and relentless. In Middleton's world the virtuous have to out-smart the wicked; and Kate believes that she had providence on her side:

> The secret powers work wondrously and duly.   (I.ii.149)

Some sympathy may be aroused for her victim, who is presumably less guilty than her first husband, but her expectations are aroused by Kate's pretence that she will be sexually demanding and then dashed after the wedding by her 'husband's' refusal to be kissed or to consummate the marriage:

> I can't abide these kissings
> ....
> Do you think y'have married only a cock-sparrow,
> And fit but for one business, like a fool?
> You shall not find it so.   (V.i.4, 11-13)

Lady Goldenfleece, moreover, although innocent, is tricked into a compromising situation with Beveril. But Kate regards her as an enemy, and her stratagem is designed to blackmail her into giving up her ill-gotten gains:

> Had I known't had been so wrongfully got,
> As I heard since, you should have had free leave
> T'have made choice of another master for't.
>   (V.i.43-5)

Lady Goldenfleece has been gratuitously insulted by her disappointed suitors (by their alterations in the wedding entertainment written by Beverill), and this too may arouse sympathy for her. She accepts the criticism of her former husband's acquisitive methods, agrees to marry Beveril and is so reconciled to Kate. By the end of the play she seems to be a suitable person — a kind of *dea ex machina* — to reveal the exchange of infants, information that enables Philip and Sandford to enjoy their respective partners.

The general reconciliation at the end is helped by Philip's purgatorial experience, when he believes he will be separated for ever by the tables of consanguinity from the girl he has married, by the very mild punishment of the vindictive suitors and by the fact that Beveril, the rescuer of Lady Twilight, and Kate's brother, loves and marries Lady Goldenfleece.

This discussion of the two plots of the play has omitted all reference to the most original scene and hardly mentioned one of the most important characters, Weatherwise. The other characters are largely determined by the plot and by the actions they have to perform; Lady Twilight, for example, has to be inhumanly forgiving; Sir Oliver has to be testy, credulous, and mean; Sir Gilbert, lecherous and treacherous. Philip had to be like the scapegrace heroes of Latin comedy and Savorwit like the cunning servants who minister to their vices. But Weatherwise, whose function in the two plots is minimal — he is an unsuccessful suitor in both — is a very entertaining character in the humors tradition. He is obsessed with almanacks and believes implicitly in their doggerel advice. Much of it is taken from Thomas Bretnor's *Prognostication*, John Dade's *New Almanacke*, Jeffery Neve's *New Almanacke and Prognostication* and Dauncy's *Almanacke* for the year 1614.[6] Although Weatherwise takes part with the other suitors in the insult to Lady Goldenfleece, he is generally good-natured, blaming his disappointments on the prognostications. When he is snubbed by Sir Oliver, who had promised him Grace in marriage, he resolves 'never to leave the love of an open-hearted widow for a narrow-eyed maid again' (I.i.295-6), and he concludes philosophically:

> My almanack told me true, how I should fare,
> Let no man think to speed against the hair.
> (I.i.301-2)

The elaborate banquet to which he invites Lady Goldenfleece in order to further his suit — it is the occasion of Kate's exposure of Sir Gilbert — is designed to match his guests with dishes decked as signs of the zodiac: Aries, Lady Goldenfleece; Taurus, Sir Gilbert; Gemini, Pepperton (because he had twins by his first wife); Cancer, Overdon — 'For when a thing's past fifty it grows crooked' (II.i.117). Weatherwise's tenants fill six other places, with strict instructions to eat little 'as you hope for new leases' (II.i.135) and to hold their tongues.

Both this scene and the entertainment of the four elements, written by Beveril and spoiled by the suitors, require elaborate staging: and Weatherwise's obsession with almanacks, which becomes tedious to read, could be very funny in the hands of a good actor.

The qualities of the play are theatrical, rather than poetical, and this has made literary critics undervalue it. One may suspect that they are shocked by the callous behaviour of Philip and by the doting imbecility of his mother. Nevertheless, it is a crowded, lively and varied comedy which does not deserve its neglect.[7]

NOTES

1. The text of the plays is based on the first editions; for convenience, the line numbering is Bullen's.
2. T.S. Elio, *Elizabethan Essays* (Faber, London 1932), p. 87.
3. See Volume XI of *The Complete Works of Algernon Charles Swinburne*, ed. Sir Edmund Grosse and Thomas J. Wise (London 1926), p. 391-406, *passim*.
4. R.H. Barker, *Thomas Middleton* (Columbia University Press: New York 1958); David M. Holmes, *The Art of Thomas Middleton* (Clarendon Press: Oxford 1970); Dorothy M. Farr, *Thomas Middleton and the Drama of Realism* (Oliver and Boyd: Edinburgh 1973).
5. Middleton's indebtedness was pointed out by D.J. Gordon, 'Middleton's *More Dissemblers besides Women* and Della Porta's *La Sorella*', 17 (1941) 400-414. There is a good account of *La Sorella* in *Italian Comedy in the Renaissance* by Marbin T. Herrick (University of Chicago Press: Chicago, 1960).

6. Pointed out by D. George, 'Weather-wise's Almanac and the Date of Middleton's *No Wit, No Help like a Woman's*', *Notes and Queries* (1966), 297-301.
7. I am indebted to members of a graduate seminar who worked on this play with me.

11

The Case of John Ford

In spite of the many books written on John Ford during the
last forty years and some notable essays by T. S. Eliot, Peter
Ure, and Robert Ornstein, his standing is still insecure. He is
contrasted, very much to his disadvantage, with Middleton,
Webster, and Tourneur. He is branded as a 'decadent', whatever moral or aesthetic decline that label implies, and we have
had little opportunity of seeing his work where it belongs — in
the theatre. It is unfortunate that some of the best and most
influential critics of our time regard the playhouse as a place of
vulgarity, where poetic conceptions, appreciated in the study,
are coarsened and perverted, and where the second-rate sometimes seems more effective than the undeniably excellent. Yet
there have been some interesting revivals of several of Ford's
plays. In 1975 the production of *Perkin Warbeck* at Stratford-
upon-Avon — though not in the Royal Shakespeare Theatre
— redeemed an otherwise undistinguished season. Some years
ago there was an open-air performance, also at Stratford, by
students of the Queen's University, Belfast, of *The Broken
Heart* and another one of the same play at the Chichester
Festival in 1962, in which Laurence Olivier played Bassanes,
and Rosemary Harris, Penthea. There have been numerous
revivals of *'Tis Pity She's a Whore* at one of which Siegfried
Sassoon, distressed by the behaviour of the audience, com-
mented that 'Mermaid Dramatists were out of fashion.' Best of
all there was a production of *The Witch of Edmonton* at the
Old Vic in 1936. This was superbly directed by Michel St.
Denis, with Edith Evans and Beatrix Lehmann in the cast. It
was a memorable and haunting experience which set a standard
for the production of Elizabethan and Jacobean plays, seldom
equalled since, and never excelled. It was splendidly poetic and
at the same time convincingly real. Some of the best scenes in

that collaborative work, it is generally agreed, were written by Ford.

Ford had doubtless suffered from Lamb's excessive praise, mingling blasphemy and bardolatry, of the scene in the last act of *The Broken Heart*, and from the disappointment with the whole play which one is likely to feel after reading Lamb's *Specimens*. He has suffered too from a belief that he indulges in gratuitous horrors, such as Giovanni's macabre entrance with Annabella's heart. His heroes seem to belong to a psycho-pathologist's casebook, and the influence on him by Burton's *Anatomy of Melancholy* has been charted by Sensabaugh and Ewing.[1] To such complaints one could retort that Lamb's excessive praise has not permanently damaged Webster's reputation, that there are gratuitous horrors in Tourneur and Middleton, and that many of the principal characters of all three dramatists could be dismissed as psychopaths — Ferdinand, Vindice and Beatrice, for example.

It is a favorite, if futile, critical exercise to compare plays by Shakespeare's forerunners and successors with his own master-pieces. It is not difficult to demonstrate triumphantly that *Macbeth*, written when Shakespeare was over forty, is superior to *Doctor Faustus*, written when Marlowe was in his twenties and written before Shakespeare, who was of the same age, had done anything as good. It is even easier to show that *'Tis Pity She's a Whore* is inferior to the play on which it is modelled, *Romeo and Juliet*. Putana corresponds to Juliet's Nurse and Bonaventura to Friar Lawrence; in place of the family feud which prevents the happiness of Shakespeare's lovers, Ford introduces the taboo of incest; and in place of Friar Lawrence's plan to avert Juliet's marriage to Paris, or the exposure of her secret marriage to Romeo, Ford substitutes Friar Bona-ventura's hope that Annabella will be cured of her incestuous passion by her marriage to Soranzo. There is a literary Gres-ham's law under which the more sensational drives out the less. Fictional lovers today apparently have to behave in ways which would have shocked Lady Chatterley and her lover. So, we are told, Caroline dramatists were compelled to appear to the sophisticated and jaded tastes of their audience by ever-increasing sensationalism; and the more the theatres were attacked by the Puritans as sinks of iniquity, the more audiences displayed the rightness of their political views by their applause at what most shocked their opponents. Whereas only one of Shakespeare's heroines breaks the seventh commandment, and the rape of Lavinia is condemned by the poet as severely as the incestuous relationship of Antiochus with his daughter, Ford's attitude to his guilty pair appears at first sight to be ambivalent, if not condoning. The lines which have been a particular stumbling block are spoken by Giovanni just before his murder of his sister:

> If ever after-times should hear
> Of our fast-knit affections, though perhaps
> The laws of conscience and of civil use
> May justly blame us, yet when they but know
> Our loves, that love will wipe away that rigour,
> Which would in other incests be abhorr'd.
>
>   (V.v.68-73)

Ford is not arguing, as has sometimes been suggested, that the sin of incest is redeemed by the mutual love of Giovanni and Annabella. He does not even make his hero put forward any such defense. Giovanni admits that conscience as well as custom will justly condemn them, but he hopes nevertheless that their love will arouse pity and mitigate the severity of their condemnation. Unlike Shelley, whose Laon and Cythna are depicted as superior to the society which condemns them, Ford merely implies that our moral disapproval should be mixed with pity. Giovanni is a brilliant student, commended by the Friar; he struggles at first, like Phèdre, against his obsession, and he is led into freethinking by a kind of defence mechanism after he and Annabella have become lovers. The Friar, although he is not entirely a spokesman for the author, is an eloquent defender of moral orthodoxy. He persuades Annabella to repent, and his dubious advice to her about marriage can be explained if not excused, as a plot-device.

  Ford's own detachment from the moral attitudes of his hero is apparent in the final scene. Giovanni's murder of Annabella is a natural conclusion to their death-marked relationship; but his entrance with her heart spitted on his dagger is not so much the dramatist's concession to the perverted taste of the audience as an indication that Giovanni has crossed the borders of madness. The play is not marred, as most of Ford's are, by feeble comic scenes. Soranzo's guilt with regard to Hippolita undercuts his moral indignation with Annabella, and his death at Giovanni's hands is acceptable to most members of an audience.

The best scenes of the play are deservedly famous, worthy to rank with any written after Shakespeare's retirement. I am thinking of the scene in which Giovanni unexpectedly finds that his passion is returned:

> *Anna.* For every sigh that thou has spent for me
> I have sigh'd ten; for every tear shed twenty
> And not so much for that I lov'd as that
> I durst not say I lov'd nor scarcely think it.
> *Giov.* Let not this music be a dream, ye gods,
> For pity's sake, I beg'ee!
> *Anna.* On my knees,
> Brother, even by our mother's dust, I charge you,
> Do not betray me to your mirth or hate,
> Love me or kill me, brother.
>
> (I.ii.244-252)

Equally famous is the scene in which Annabella is murdered, with Giovanni denying, and his sister affirming, the existence of heaven and hell. But there are other scenes which are equally brilliant, notably the one in which Giovanni defends his conduct to the Friar and the spine-chilling episode in which the loyal villain, Vasques, extracts the name of Annabella's lover from Putana and then has her gagged and blinded. *'Tis Pity She's a Whore* is Ford's most effective stage-play, although there are scenes in other plays which show his poetical quality to better advantage.

II

The Lover's Melancholy is a case in point. The play as a whole is a comparative failure. It is flawed by the boringly comic scenes concerned with Cuculus; and, even if these were regarded as detachable excrescences, by the slowness of the earlier acts, which is hardly alleviated by the momentary jealousy of Menaphon. The play moreover is filled with echoes of Shakespeare.

Thamasta falls in love with Parthenophil, the disguised Eroclea, in much the same way that Olivia falls in love with
Cesario. Both disguised girls make eloquent appeals for the
men who love Thamasta and Olivia, but both Menaphon and
Orsino accuse them of treachery. (Ford confuses matters here,
since Menaphon has watched unseen Parthenophil's rejection
of Thamasta's advances.) The madness of Meleander distinctly
recalls Lear's, and Cleophila, his dutiful daughter, is reminis-
cent of Cordelia. As Clifford Leech observes [2], when Meleander
is arrayed in fresh garments while asleep, there seems to be an
echo of the scene in which Lear recovers. The cause of
Meleander's madness, however, is not ingratitude, but the
attempted rape by the king of his other daughter, Eroclea, and
her flight into exile.

The other apparent imitation of Shakespeare is in Act 4, in
which the gradual recognition of Eroclea by Palador owes a
great deal to the plays of Shakespeare's last period, in particular to the recognition of Marina by Pericles. There are, however, significant differences. Pericles believes that Marina is
dead, and she is not aware of his identity: the gradualness of
the recognition is therefore plausible. In Ford's play, on the
other hand, Eroclea is fully aware of Palador's identity, and
Palador, despite broad hints, is slow to recognize that Parthenophil is Eroclea. Even when she appears in female garments, he
supposes her to be an imposter. We are meant to understand
that Palador's 'melancholy' — the neurosis caused by his
separation from the woman he loves — makes him unable to
believe what he wishes to believe, since he feels it is too good to
be true. This recognition scene contains some of Ford's finest
poetry.

Eliot, who called attention to the influence of the plays of
Shakespeare's final period, complained that although 'Ford is
struck by the dramatic and poetic effectiveness of the situation,
[he] uses it on a level hardly higher than that of the device of
twins in comedy' [3]. Eliot allowed that this scene and the
recognition by Meleander in Act 5 were 'well planned and well
written, and [were] even moving'; but, he argued, compared
with Shakespeare's the scenes failed. Ford, Beaumont and
Fletcher 'had no conception of what he was trying to do; they
speak another and cruder language. In their poetry there is no

symbolic value ... it is poetry and drama of the surface'. These comments seem to me to be true of Beaumont and Fletcher, but quite unjust to Ford. David L. Frost is nearer the truth when he says that in this play Ford 'shows signs of having found in Shakespeare inspiration as well as exploitable material'. For in these two scenes he displayed a realization of what Shakespeare was doing in *Pericles* and *Cymbeline*. The ritual of restoration and recognition in the last acts of those two plays is repeated in *The Lover's Melancholy*, but without any slavish imitation of Shakespeare. It could indeed be said that Shakespeare had to wait for three centuries before the critics caught up with Ford's insight. Eliot was constrained to admit that Ford, 'though intermittently, was able to manipulate sequences of words in blank verse in a manner which is quite his own'. One is tempted to echo a line in *Four Quartets*: 'That was a way of putting it — not very satisfactory'. Unsatisfactory, because the ability to write blank verse which is unlike that of any other poet is not primarily a matter of technique. The cadences of Ford's blank verse are a reflection of his imaginative perception of reality. We need not deny that he had absorbed *The Anatomy of Melancholy* (as modern poets have absorbed Freud), but it is fairly certain that he found in Burton's attitude to his case histories a confirmation of his previously formed attitudes toward love and life.

The reunion of Palador and Eroclea, foreseen by the audience from the first act of the play, and delayed mainly by Palador's depressive illness, as well as by the business of Thamasta's infatuation, which enables us to know Euroclea better, does not depend for its effect on the element of surprise. (No audience is surprised by the score of 'surprises' in the last scene of *Cymbeline*.) The early part of the reunion scene is slow and meditative, introduced by Palador's wish to see the lost Parthenophil: 'For he is like to something I remember/A great while since, a long, long time ago'. His soliloquy is continued by Eroclea, who enters in the middle of it; and this has the effect of showing their compatibility, as when Mirabel continues Millamant's quotation from Waller. Palador's assumption that Parthenophil is disguised as Eroclea, and not the other way around, and his tardiness is acknowledging the truth may be ascribed to his feeling that

man is 'fortune's exercise', and as I have suggested, to his
inability to believe in happiness. In the end he is brought to
accept it:

> We are but fools
> To trifle in disputes, or vainly struggle
> With that eternal mercy which protects us.
> Come home, home to my heart, thou banished peace!
>
> (IV.iii)

The peace is, of course, embodied in Eroclea.

The last act, which is almost as impressive, contains a
sequence of happy events. Cleophila reconciles Thamasta and
Menaphon, Thamasta reciprocates by bringing Amethus and
Cleophila together, and Eroclea is reunited with her sister.
There follows the 'cordial' administered to Meleander — first
as in *King Lear* and *Pericles*, music; then Aretus with a patent
restoring the old man to his former honors, together with
additional ones; then Sophronos with a portrait of Eroclea;
then Eroclea herself; and lastly Palador, who claims Eroclea as
his bride.

The Lover's Melancholy was Ford's first unaided play;
but already it displays his ability to absorb the work of his
predecessors while introducing an original and distinctive note
into the drama of the period.

III

Another play which was partly inspired by Shakespeare is
Love's Sacrifice, and in this case Ford's model was *Othello*. The
villain, Roderico d'Avolos, blurts out remarks which are calculated to arouse the duke's suspicions (such as Iago's "I like not
that";) and then he accused Bianca with an Iago-like show of
reluctance. The Duke's accusations of Bianca and the struggle
in his mind between jealousy and trust contain verbal echoes of
Shakespeare's play. But Ford appears to have wished to 'improve' on *Othello* by removing such supposed deficiencies as
later critics found in the play — that Iago is a demidevil or a
stage villain or a mere dramatic mechanism; that the handker-

chief is flimsy evidence of adultery; that Desdemona could not have committed the 'act of shame' a thousand times in the time at her disposal; and that Othello would have accused Desdemona much earlier. D'Avolos is not a mere dramatic mechanism, and he has an understandable motive. He wishes to gain advancement by pleasing Fiormonda, who hates Fernando for repulsing her advances and hates Bianca for being her successful rival. D'Avolos, in spite of his corrupt motive, does honestly believe that Fernando and Bianca have committed adultery: their behavior is enough to arouse anyone's suspicions and provides apparent ocular proof. D'Avolos, therefore, does not have to rely on a purloined handkerchief, a fabricated dream or the timely arrival of Cassio's mistress — who shares a name with Ford's heroine. Indeed D'Avolos's guilt is so much minimized that the reader may feel inclined to protest at the severity of the sentence which is passed upon him:

> Convey him to the prison's top; in chains
> Hang him alive; whosoe'er lends a bit
> Of bread to feed him, dies.
>
> (V.iii.145-7)

The Duke's jealousy is made plausible and, despite Ford's intention, even justified, by the extraordinary behavior of Bianca and Fernando. Fernando gives himself away to D'Avolos by his reactions to Bianca's portrait. He confesses his love to her on several occasions until she threatens to tell her husband. He promises never to mention the subject again; but the very same night she comes in a nightgown to his bedroom, confesses that she returns his love, exchanges passionate kisses and swears to commit suicide if he proceeds to seduce her. Later, when other people are present, she proposes to steal a kiss. She invites Fernando to her bed-chamber, and they are caught (as it appears) in *flagrante delicto* by the Duke, D'Avolos, and Fiormonda. Fernando is led away, and Bianca, in an attempt to save his life and (as Clifford Leech thinks) in order to provoke the Duke to kill her, declares that she had tried unsuccessfully to seduce him. We can see however that the platonic relationship to which she had restricted him was not as innocent as she imagines and that she deserves neither the tribute of Fernando

nor that of the duke. She is not 'as free of lust/As any terms of
art can deify', nor can her tomb be properly described as a
'shrine of fairest purity'. Ford's own attitude is ambiguous.
On the one hand he seems to have believed that there was an
absolute moral difference between Bianca's platonic passion
and adultery; on the other hand he revealed, perhaps in-
advertently, that she was playing with fire, that she was a
sexual tease and that she was a self-deceiver. In spite of the
contemporary cult of platonic love, Donne and the Cavalier
poets were all aware of the 'right true end of love' and of the
ease with which followers of this cult might end up in bed. The
critics, not unnaturally, have disagreed about how the play
should be interpreted. Peter Ure argued that Bianca was 'not a
true initiate of the platonic cult', whereas Fernando was.
Cifford Leech denies the possibility of this interpretation.
Neither critic, I think, appreciates the element of self-
deception in Bianca's character, and one sympathizes with
Robert Ornstein's comment on Bianca's speeches to the Duke
in Act 5 Scene 1: 'We cannot decide whether she is an innocent
posing as a wanton, or a wanton posing as an innocent acting the
part of a wanton'.

There is a curious underplot in which three women, seduced
and made pregnant by Ferentes, conspire to murder him during
a dance. They apparently escape punishment, and the abbot
comments: 'Tis just/He dies by murder that hath lived in lust'.
Presumably the unplatonic behavior of the three women is
meant to contrast with that of the lovers of the main plot and to
show that Bianca's technical chastity deserves our admiration.
But Ford fumbles as much in the underplot as in the main plot.

IV

The Broken Heart contains some of Ford's finest dramatic
poetry and his most moving scenes, but it is structurally
unsatisfactory. Two points will illustrate this. In Act 2 Ithocles
asks Prophilus to conduct Penthea to the palace gardens as he
wishes to talk with her. Penthea is duly conducted to the
rendezvous, and then Prophilus leaves her with the disguised
Orgilus, with the request: 'Do thy best/To make this lady

merry for an hour'. Ithocles, we are told later, has been carried to his closet after he has had a sudden fit. Ford makes Prophilus behave in this absurd way and introduces Ithocles' illness as a clumsy device to enable Penthea and Orgilus to meet. The other structural flaw is more significant. The broken heart of the title is Calantha, whose death in the last scene exemplifies her words — a variation on a famous line of Seneca's: 'They are the silent griefs which cut the heart strings'. In the previous scene she had been informed, during a formal dance, of the deaths of her father and Penthea and of the murder of the man she loves. She continues the dance, apparently unmoved; and although this scene is superb in itself, it is not quite as effective in its place in the play.

The difficulty facing a director is that until Act 5 Calantha has not been a central character and, apart from the scene in which Penthea pleads her brother's cause, she has not made much impression. During the first four acts our interest has been focused on Penthea, whose heart too is broken, though in her case the process is prolonged. Her feeling that her marriage to Bassanes is prostitution, since she had been betrothed to Orgilus, leads eventually to madness and what is virtually suicide. We see her in relation to her jealous husband, to her lover and to the brother who has forced her to marry a man whom she does not love. Although her name means 'complaint' she does not complain of her treatment by Bassanes. What she does complain of through the play, to both Orgilus and Ithocles, is her unwilling 'adultery'. She forgives her brother in the end and ensures that Calantha will return his love.

All through the first four acts, therefore, our interest is concentrated on Penthea and on the three men with whom she is involved: Orgilus, who is anxious to avenge himself on Ithocles, but who is ready to commit almost the same sin by claiming the right to veto his own sister's marriage; Ithocles, who is now a national hero and repents his interference with Penthea's happiness, even though his love for Calantha is mixed with ambition; and Bassanes, whose jealousy is exacerbated by his realization that his love is not returned. All three men are deeply flawed but not ignoble: Orgilus, even in the act of revenge to which he is driven more by Penthea's suffering than by his own wrongs, pays tribute to his enemy; and Ithocles magnanimously forgives him.

Penthea's laments could easily have become monotonous: they are saved from that by variations of tone (resignation, anger, indignation, shame), by the way they modulate into madness and by the use of music and ritual. The offstage dirge to mark Penthea's passing and her veiled corpse seated between Orgilus and Ithocles are two of Ford's finest inventions. He avoids, if narrowly, the sentimentality with which Fletcher decorates Aspatia in *The Maid's Tragedy* and the jailor's daughter in *The Two Noble Kinsmen*; and one has only to compare Penthea's madness with Belvidera's — both of them more stylized than Ophelia's — to see Ford's enormous superiority in tact, taste, and poetic quality. What is particularly notable is the subtle mingling of sense and delusion, which both reflect her sense of outrage:

> No falsehood
> Equals a broken faith; there's not a hair
> Sticks on my head but, like a leaden plummet,
> It sinks me to the grave: I must creep thither;
> The journey is not long.
>
> (IV.ii.75-9)

In her next speech Penthea begins by regretting her childlessness:

> I might have been
> Mother to many pretty prattling babes;
> They would have smil'd when I smil'd, and for certain
> I should have cried when they cried.

A few lines later she forgets the existence of her husband and that she is still young: ''Tis too late for me to marry now,/I am past child-bearing'. She takes Orgilus's hand and kisses it, and then speaks the most haunting lines in the play:

> Remember
> When we last gather'd roses in the garden,
> I found my wits; but truly you lost yours.

Before the end of the scene Penthea recovers sufficiently to say that her honour has been ruined by:

> A cruel brother and a desperate dotage!
> There is no peace left for a ravish'd wife
> Widow'd by lawless marriage.

She resolves — and in this resolution she is depicted as sane — to starve herself to death. Every scene in which Penthea appears — her martyrdom with Bassanes, her heart-rending scene with Orgilus, her forgiveness of Ithocles, her bequest to Calantha — exhibits Ford at his best.

V

Ford's other plays, with one exception, are disappointing. *The Lady's Trial* and *The Fancies Chaste and Noble* are inferior to the plays already discussed. The exception, *Perkin Warbeck*, is a remarkable play, quite unlike Ford's other work and unlike any plays written at this time. It is a well-plotted tragic history which keeps generally close to the known facts. Where Ford deviates from his sources it is to increase our sympathy for the hero. The historical Warbeck confessed before his death that he was an imposter, and the historical Katherine married again three times. Ford's Warbeck does not confess, and his Katherine swears 'to die a faithful widow' to his bed.

The play is notable for its sympathetic portraits of the kings of Scotland and England. James IV supports Warbeck as long as he can and refuses to buy peace with his blood. Henry VII, who has been lenient to an earlier imposter, Lambert Simnel, is shown as deeply shocked by Stanley's treason and is afraid to see him after the discovery lest he should pardon him. He puts down the rebellion with the minimum of bloodshed, and he pities the misguided rebels:

> Alas, poor souls! let such as are escaped
> Steal to the country back without pursuit;
> There's not a drop of blood spilt, but hath drawn
> As much of mine.
>
> (III.i.82-5)

He would even have pardoned Warbeck if he had admitted that he was an imposter. Another example of Ford's even-handed justice is the impressive scene between the traitor Stanley and the informer Clifford.

Despite this ability to see events from both sides, it would seem that Ford's imagination was most engaged in the scenes in which the pretender appears. Inspired, perhaps, by the loyalty and devotion of Katherine (who nevertheless does not say whether she believes in his claim) or by the psychological problem of the self-deceiver, Ford's style is noticeably finer in these scenes. It has been argued by Mark Stavig in *John Ford and the Traditional Moral Order* [4] that 'since the imagery throughout the play has stressed the association of Perkin with witchcraft and the devil and of Henry with heaven and the forces of good, it does not seem improper to accept Urswick's analysis of Perkin's madness'. But Warbeck's opponents natur- ally ascribe his persuasiveness to witchcraft, as Brabantio accused Othello of winning Desdemona in this way; and the total impression left by the play is quite different. Warbeck is continually shielded by the poetry Ford puts into his mouth. He speaks and behaves as a prince and dies like a hero:

> Heaven be obeyed!
> Impoverish time of its amazement, friends,
> And we will prove as trusty in our payments,
> As prodigal to nature in our debts.
> Death? pish! 'tis but a sound; a name of air;
> A minute's storm, or not so much; to tumble
> From bed to bed, be massacred alive
> By some physicians, for a month or two,
> In the hope of freedom from a fever's torments,
> Might stagger manhood; here the pain is past
> Ere sensibly 'tis felt. Be men of spirit!
> Spurn coward passion! so illustrious mention
> Shall blaze our names, and style us kings o'er Death.
>   (V.iii)

Ford avoided an easy contrast of noble imposter with ignoble ruler. Henry VII is depicted more sympathetically than by most historians. Nevertheless, we are posed with the question: Is not a man who behaves like a prince and dies heroically a hero and a 'prince'? Like a character in a Pirandello play, or like Argia in Betti's *The Queen and the Rebels*, Warbeck becomes the prince he imagines himself to be. Although the play stands outside the main line of Ford's dramas, it is in some ways the most modern in spirit of all his writings.

All Ford's plays are seriously flawed: but that *Perkin Warbeck* has fewest defects does not make it his masterpiece, as Eliot perversely argued. His more characteristic plays are concerned with the aberrations of sexual passion, and this forms a link with the dreary didactic poem *Christ's Bloody Sweat*, in which poets are blamed for disguising lust as love, and thereby drawing 'whole troopes of soules to hell'. Critics have expressed surprise that the author of that poem should afterwards write the plays for which he is famous; but the plays exemplify in their different ways what happens when passion dominates reason. Ford did not agree with Antony that the nobleness of life was to do thus. The desperate ends of Giovanni, Bianca, Orgilus and Ithocles, no less than the undeserved suffering of Penthea and Calantha, illustrate his moral position. The religious tone of the early poem has been modified by the lessons of psychology, many of his characters being diseased rather than wicked; and the Christian ideas have been modified too, as in so many tragic writers, by stoicism. The virtuous characters may meet with misfortune and tragedy through the faults of others, their hearts may break, but they retain their integrity. Ford contrasts the good and the great, as Stavig and Oliver have shown, and in a passage salvaged by Oliver from the manuscript of *The Line of Life* we may be tempted to find the centre of Ford's dramatic persona. He is showing how the true glory of a virtuous man survives the accidents and disasters of life:[5]

Howsoever he live, sequestered from commerce by the injustice of a prevailing enemy; or shut up in prison by the suggestion of nimble information; or disgraced by the credulous confidence of misinformed majesty; or despised by the many-tongued malice of the abused multitude; or impoverished by the oppression of an ever-begging, but a never satisfied, flattery; or defamed by the graceless rumour of scandal; or traduced by the puzzling deceit and snare or smooth imposture; or — which is the finishing of mischiefs and miseries — put to death by the importunity of the faulty.

John Ford was perhaps more certain of the accidents and disasters than he was of 'the richest chain wherewith a good man can be adorned', namely the '*via lactea* of immortality in his name on earth'; but this was the core of his philosophy of life.

NOTES

1. G. F. Sensabagh, *The Tragic Muse of John Ford* (Stanford, 1954); S. B. Ewing, *Burtonian Melancholy in the plays of John Ford* (Princeton, 1946).
2. Clifford Leech, *John Ford and the drama of his time* (Chatto and Windus: London, 1957).
3. Cf. p. 183 below.
4. Mark Stavig, *John Ford and the traditional moral order* (Madison, Wisc., 1968).
5. H. J. Oliver, *The Problem of John Ford* (Melbourne, 1955).

12

T. S. Eliot's Criticism of Elizabethan Drama

A great poet's criticism is always valuable, however much it is designed to defend his own practice. Wordsworth's preface to the *Lyrical Ballads,* for example, although obviously unjust to eighteenth-century poets, was a necessary apologia for his own style of poetry. Eliot, although he never wrote a preface to his own poems, defended them indirectly in much of his criticism. It was necessary for him to establish the superiority of the metaphysicals to the poets of the nineteenth century and to tumble Milton from his pedestal if his own verse was to find acceptance. He was, moreover, interested in reviving poetic drama, while realizing that it was essential to escape from the influence of Shakespeare, an influence which had frustrated the efforts of so many poets of the previous century. One has only to think of the poets of the Romantic period with their closet dramas — *Remorse, The Borderers, Cain, The Cenci, Otho the Great* — and the plays of Tennyson, Browning, Swinburne, Bridges and Stephen Philips, to realize the baleful effects of Shakespeare's greatness. It is significant that the only lines quoted in 'Tradition and the Individual Talent' (1917), the earliest of the *Selected Essays,* are the famous ones from *The Revenger's Tragedy,* the cadences of which were echoed in Eliot's own poetry. In the following year he attacked Gilbert Murray's translations of Euripides, not merely because he turned Greek lyric into 'the fluid haze of Swinburne', but also because they served as a bad model for anyone wishing to revive poetic drama.

'A Dialogue on Dramatic Poetry', which belongs to the same period as *Sweeney Agonistes,* purports to be a conversation between seven men, who are given letters, not names, and who are not properly differentiated, as Dryden's brilliantly are. Indeed, all the seven seem to express Eliot's own views, or at least dramatic exaggerations of his actual opinions. It is said that plays should do more than amuse; that the moral attitude of *Mr Limberham* is impeccable; that ballet is valuable because it concerns itself with permanent form; that the perfect and ideal drama is to be found in the ceremony of the Mass; that if we want to get at the permanent and universal we tend to express ourselves in verse; that the poet in Shaw was stillborn; that Shakespeare's plays are not morally edifying;[1] that we must find a new form of verse which will be as satisfactory a vehicle for us as Blank Verse was for the Elizabethans; that the unities of Place and Time will be found highly desirable for the drama of the future; and 'I am a member of the Labour Party'. Of these ten remarks, spoken by five characters, only the last seems not to be Eliot's; and even this is in the context of praise of Ernie Lotinga — a praise which is directly comparable to Eliot's eulogy of Marie Lloyd, written five years before. The ostensible purpose of the dialogue was to discuss the possibility of modern poetic drama. In the year when it was written there were a number of active poetic dramatists — Yeats, Bottomley, Binyon, Masefield — and that Eliot does not mention any one of them is an indication that he regarded their work as largely irrelevant to the future of poetic drama.[2]

It should be mentioned that when Eliot began to write on Elizabethan drama, the two most influential books were probably Bradley's *Shakespearean Tragedy* and Dowden's *Shakspere: A Critical Study of his Mind and Art,* in which he attempted to relate Shakespeare's tragic period ('in the depths') to events in his life. Those critics who rebelled against Bradley and Dowden, and reacted against the praise of Elizabethan drama by Lamb and Swinburne, either treated the poetry of the plays as irrelevant to the dramatic effect (Archer) or exposed the apparent inconsistencies in Shakespeare's characterization (Stoll) or in his 'primitive' technique (Schücking) or blamed his defects on his incorporation of material from source plays (Robertson).

Eliot's central position on Elizabethan drama is to be found in 'Four Elizabethan Dramatists', a preface to a book he never wrote. The dramatists are Webster, Tourneur, Middleton and Chapman, none of them precisely Elizabethan. In this essay he points out that one should not approach these dramatists by way of Lamb's *Specimens*, nor through Archer's *The Old Drama and the New*. Lamb separated the poetry from the theatre — he could hardly have done anything else at the beginning of the nineteenth century; and Archer notoriously deplored poetry as irrelevant to drama. Yet Eliot was more under the influence of Lamb and Archer than he was aware. He laments the 'impure art' of the dramatists, including Shakespeare's and suggests that only in *Everyman* was English drama free from the foolish pursuit of realism. 'The weakness of Elizabethan drama', he asserts, 'is not its defect of realism, but its attempts at realism, not its conventions, but its lack of conventions'. To this one can say only that all the better dramatists did not attempt realism but merely tried to arouse in the audience the illusion of realism; and, as Muriel Bradbrook demonstrated in her first two books, they all used conventions.[3] When Eliot goes on to say that Henry Arthur Jones and Shakespeare are 'essentially of the same type' and that both are 'to be read rather than seen', he is being deliberately provocative: the life of Jones' plays is in the theatre, and only in the theatre, and all the Elizabethan dramatists relied on the collaboration of the players to realize their intentions.

The 'general philosophy of life' to be found in Shakespeare and his contemporaries is summarized by Santayana (with Eliot's approval in this essay) in the statement that 'Duncan is in his grave'. As a summary of the philosophical position of any of the seven or eight major dramatists of the period, it is as manifestly inept as only a bad epigram can be. Nor can it be said that Webster is 'a great literary and dramatic genius directed towards chaos'. Here, as elsewhere, Eliot seems to confuse the views of characters in a play with those of the author. The same confusion is apparent in another essay when he subscribes to Cunliffe's observation on the hopeless fatalism of *King Lear* as evidenced, not as one might suppose by Kent's 'It is the stars' or Edgar's 'Ripeness is all', but by Gloucester's words:

As flies to wanton boys are we to the gods:

They kill us for their sport.

This is an appropriate exclamation of a superstitious old man who is suffering both mental and physical agony; but we should remember that not long afterwards Gloucester prays, without irony, to the 'ever-gentle gods'. Both sentiments are in character and neither can be regarded as the expression of the poet's considered beliefs.[4] Eliot again quotes Gloucester's lines and goes on to speak of 'Shakespeare's general cynicism and disillusionment'. It is significant, perhaps, that in the same essay Eliot refers warmly to Wyndham Lewis' *The Lion and the Fox*, a book that expresses similar views about Shakespeare's pessimism.[5] Now when Thomas Hardy declared that the President of the Immortals had finished his sport with Tess, we can accept this as the novelist's own vision of life; but when Macbeth tells us that life is a tale 'told by an idiot, signifying nothing', this merely expresses the private hell of the protagonist rather than the poet's own philosophy of life. Shakespeare, of course, uses many choric figures, and there are many passages which have a choric effect — remarks by Edgar. Kent and Enobarbus, for example — but we should never imagine that characters of whom the poet clearly disapproves express his own views.[6] Anyone who writes tragedies has to adopt a tragic stance, whatever his private beliefs and temperament.

Three of Eliot's four chosen dramatists have frequently been revived in recent years. The persevering playgoer has had reasonable opportunities of seeing productions of Middleton, Webster and Tourneur; but Chapman, whom Eliot regarded as 'potentially perhaps the greatest artist of all these men', has been given a wide berth by professional directors. The terms of Eliot's praise are revealing; Chapman, he says:

> was the mind which was the most classical, his was the drama which is the most independent in its tendency toward a dramatic form — although it may seem the most formless and the most indifferent to dramatic necessities.

This is virtually an admission that the tragedies of Bussy and Byron, however attractive the poetry contained in them, are not really good acting plays. Chapman's real masterpieces are a handful of comedies, of which *The Widow's Tears* is the best. Eliot had already echoed Chapman in one of his own poems,[7] but his remarks exhibit the literary bias of his dramatic criticism at this time. He quotes more than once the same great speech from *The Revenger's Tragedy,* and one is driven to suspect that here too he is much less interested in the drama as a whole than in the more or less detachable poetic speeches.[8]

As early as 1919 Eliot had spoken of the way Elizabethan drama had:

> grown away from the rhetorical expression, the bombast speeches of Kyd and Marlowe to the subtle and dispersed utterance of Shakespeare and Webster.

It is dangerous to equate rhetoric and bombast. Shakespeare continued to use all the resources of rhetoric throughout his career, though with increasing subtlety. 'Pray you, undo this button' and 'No cause, no cause' are so effective only because their simplicity contrasts with the rhetorical tirades of the storm scenes.[9] Eliot, however, argues that Shakespeare's 'really fine rhetoric' is to be found, and only to be found, 'in situations where a character in a play sees himself in a dramatic light'. He quotes examples from *Othello, Timon of Athens,* and *Coriolanus*: and when eight years later he wrote on 'Shakespeare and the Stoicism of Seneca', he referred again to Othello's last speech, suggested that the Moor is cheering himself up, ceasing to think of Desdemona, and endeavouring to escape reality. What Eliot calls *bovarysme* and what Leavis was later to call 'self-approving self-dramatization' has been echoed by a number of later critics; but, even apart from the fact that Othello acknowledges that he has damned himself by his crime and that he welcomes eternal punishment in hell, Eliot seems here to be confusing dramatization and self-dramatization. Characters in a play are made to project themselves, not because they are particularly egotistical but simply because the dramatist wishes to be understood.

The essay on 'Seneca in Elizabethan Translation' probably exaggerates the influence of Seneca. More recent critics have argued persuasively that the development of Elizabethan drama would not have been vastly different if all Seneca's plays had been lost.[10] In this essay and in *The Use of Poetry and the Use of Criticism*, Eliot writes in defence of the English academic Senecans who had followed Sidney's advice and thereby forfeited a popular audience. Daniel, Greville and the others, however attractive they intermittently are, are essentially undramatic. One has the feeling that Eliot believed that if only the great Elizabethans had followed Sidney's precepts, they might have created a classical drama as impressive as that of Corneille or Racine, instead of the impure art which was all they could achieve. Many readers of this essay, with its enthusiastic praise of the Jasper Heywood translations, have been disappointed when they have found that there are very few passages as good as those Eliot quotes; and even the charming lines from *Hercules Furens*, described by Eliot as 'perfect' and 'of singular beauty' are marred by the awkward syntax of the first three lines:

> Goe hurtles soules, whom mischiefe hath opprest
> Even in first porch of life but lately had,
> And fathers fury goe unhappy kind
> O little children, by the way ful sad
>   Of journey knowen.
>   Goe see the angry kynges.
>
> (Ed. Eliot, I.45)

As for the other essay in which Eliot argues that Shakespearian tragedy was influenced by the stoicism of Seneca — though Possum-like he admits that he does not believe his own thesis — this is flawed by his reluctance to recognize 'that Shakespeare's ethic is Christian, and Seneca's is not'.[11] G. K. Hunter is right to emphasize the central importance of this distinction.

In the essay on *Hamlet*, which contains the notorious comment that the play was 'certainly an artistic failure', Eliot refers to books by J. M. Robertson and Edgar Elmer Stoll. He was plainly influenced by Robertson's disintegrating attempts and by Stoll's attacks on Shakespeare's artistic integrity. It was probably from Robertson that he got the idea that the scenes between Polonius and Laertes, and between Polonius and Reynaldo were inexcusable, and certainly from Robertson that he took the idea that 'the essential emotion of the play is the feeling of a son towards a guilty mother'. This is a gratuitous assumption; and even if it were true, Hamlet's emotion is not 'in excess of the facts as they appear'. After all, Gertrude is certainly an adultress, and she is suspected of being an accomplice in the murder of her husband. Eliot's criticism of the play is based on the assumption that Shakespeare 'could ' not drag to light, contemplate, or manipulate into art' some 'stuff' from his own experience. 'Under compulsion of what experience he attempted to express the inexpressibly horrible, we shall never know'. We shall never even know if there is any foundation for this theory; but it fits in with Eliot's belief that Shakespeare:

> was occupied with the struggle — which alone constitutes life for a poet — to transmute his personal and private agonies into something rich and strange, something universal and impersonal.[12]

In *Hamlet*, Eliot thought, Shakespeare had failed to achieve this. No doubt Eliot himself had been occupied with such a struggle when he wrote *The Waste Land*, but that poem seems to have been designed to express such a struggle, whereas the emotions of *Hamlet* were largely evoked by the tale which Shakespeare inherited. Whether the early *Hamlet* was Kyd's or another's, the murder of Hamlet's father and the marriage of his mother to the murderer were the basic materials with which Shakespeare had to deal. Any dramatist would have been bound to concern himself with the reactions of the son to the mother's guilt — and he had no need of Freud to suggest to him how the subject might be treated. It may be, as Hunter suggested, that Eliot was trying to create a symbolist Shakespeare and that this fact accounts for his dissatisfaction with *Hamlet*.[13]

By 1930, when he wrote a preface to Wilson Knight's *The Wheel of Fire*, Eliot had modified his position and he was speaking of the figure in the carpet, 'the sense of a unifying pattern below the level of explicit statement'.[14] In 1950, in *Poetry and Drama*, Eliot gave an admirable analysis of the first scene of *Hamlet* and, chastened perhaps by his own experience of dramatic writing, he no longer regarded that play as an artistic failure. There are two fine unpublished lectures on the plays of the final period and, scattered through his essays, there are many perceptive remarks about Shakespeare, including three pages in 'The Music of Poetry'. As Hunter wittily suggests, Eliot 'virtually invented the twentieth-century Shakespeare in a collection of asides'.[15] In this regard we may instance the Preface to *The Wheel of Fire*, five or six remarks in the Dante essay or, here, a passage in the essay on John Ford, questionable as it is:

> The whole of Shakespeare's work is *one* poem; and it is the poetry of it in this sense, not the poetry of isolated lines and passages or the poetry of single figures which he created, that mattered most.

He had come to realize the qualities which a good critic of Shakespeare could possess. He outlined them in his introduction to Henry Fluchère's *Shakespeare* (1933):

> The ideal Shakespeare critic should be a scholar, with knowledge not of Shakespeare in isolation but of Shakespeare in relation to the Elizabethan Theatre.... and of that Theatre in relation to the social, political, economic and religious conditions of its time. He should also be a poet; and he should be a 'man of the theatre'. And he should also have a philosophic mind.

In a later introduction, to S. L. Bethell's *Shakespeare and the Popular Dramatic Tradition* (1944), Eliot recognizes the importance of performance:

> The constant reader of Shakespeare should be also, to the best of his opportunities the constant theatre-goer; for any play of Shakespeare requires to be seen and heard, as well as read, many times; and seen and heard in as many different productions as possible.

He also recognizes, more clearly than before, the nature of poetic drama:

> A verse play is not a play done into verse, but a different kind of play: in a way more realistic than 'naturalistic drama', because, instead of clothing nature in poetry, it should remove the surface of things, expose the underneath, or the inside of the natural

surface experience. It may allow the characters to behave inconsistently, but only with respect to a deeper consistency. It may use any device to show their real feelings and volitions, instead of just what, in actual life, they would normally profess or be conscious of; it must reveal, underneath the vacillating or infirm character, the indomitable unconscious will; and underneath the resolute purpose of the planning animal, the victim of circumstance and the doomed or sanctified being.

The best of Eliot's essays on Shakespeare's contemporaries contain striking insights and what seem now to be curious faults of emphasis, and even misunderstandings. The Marlowe essay, for example, makes the point, original in its time (1918), that *The Jew of Malta* is a farce rather than a tragedy; but he says little about *Doctor Faustus* and nothing at all about *Edward II* and *Hero and Leander,* arguably Marlowe's masterpiece. He seems, moreover, to imply that *Dido* was written at the end of Marlowe's life.

The essay on Middleton is one of the most persuasive. To it we owe the generally accepted view of *The Changeling* that 'in the moral essence of tragedy it is safe to say that . . . . Middleton is surpassed by one Elizabethan alone'. Nothing could be better than Eliot's account of Beatrice's development:

> she becomes moral only by becoming damned . . . . But what constitutes the essence of the tragedy is something which has not been sufficiently remarked; it is the *habituation* of Beatrice to her sin; it becomes no longer merely sin but custom . . . . The tragedy of Beatrice is not that she has lost Alsemero . . . . it is that she has won De Flores.

Nevertheless, we may feel that by concentrating on a single character Eliot ignores the tragedy of De Flores, the whole of the underplot and Middleton's collaboration with Rowley. The danger of concentrating on a single character is again apparent in Eliot's remarks on *The Roaring Girl,* and it becomes more serious in his perfunctory treatment of *Women Beware Women,* in which his interest is centred on Bianca. He declares that she 'is a type of women who is purely moved by vanity'. This ignores her original love for her husband, for whom she embraces comparative poverty, and her genuine resistance to the Duke. Even stranger is the fact that Eliot makes no mention of Isabella, and strangest of all that he does not even mention the central character of the play, Livia, who brings about the downfall and damnation of the other two women.[16]

Eliot recognizes that Middleton is 'in flashes' a great poet, a master of versification. He quotes Beatrice's final speech — with the old Mermaid misprint — as an example. He had previously imitated its rhythms in 'Gerontion'.[17] He says little about the city comedies and does not mention *A Chaste Maid in Cheapside* or that masterly study of hypocrisy, *More Dissemblers Besides Women*. When he declares that Middleton had no message, that he was merely a recorder, it is difficult to agree. From *The Wisdom of Solomon Paraphrased*, written at the age of seventeen, to *A Game of Chess*, Middleton was consistently didactic. In his lightest comedies and in his gloomiest tragedies he analyses the corruption of society from a Calvinistic viewpoint. Allwit is funny, but damned; Dampit is damned, and the humour of the scenes in which he appears is black indeed. The Cardinal, who points the moral in *Women Beware Women*, is not an irrelevant intruder, as George Hibbard used to argue. If Middleton's young prodigals and harlots arouse our sympathy and are let off lightly at the end of the plays, it is because they are less wicked than the people they cheat. So Eliot's idea of Middleton's impersonality and facelessness cannot be substantiated; and this opinion is the more surprising when juxtaposed with the statement that 'Chapman has become a breezy British character as firm as Nelson or Wellington'. Was Eliot thinking of the author of *Bussy D'Ambois*, of the Rival Poet of the Sonnets, or of the translator of Homer? Perhaps he was recalling Keats's epithets for Chapman, 'loud and bold'. In any case, 'breezy' is the last epithet to apply to Chapman.

The essays on Heywood, Tourneur, Massinger and Marston were reviews, but none the worse for that. The Tourneur essay contains Eliot's finest account of the verse of *The Revenger's Tragedy*. The essay on Massinger has some good pages on his indebtedness to Shakespeare (based on Cruickshank's book) and some excellent appreciation of the masterly structure of his blank verse, marred only by a characteristic hit at Milton's.

The Marston essay is noteworthy for the curious judgement that *Sophonisba* was his masterpiece.

Eliot was probably right to suggest that *Perkin Warbeck* and *The Broken Heart* were Ford's best plays and that his greatest quality was his ability 'to manipulate sequences of words in blank verse in a manner which is quite his own'. We may feel that his characterization of Giovanni as 'almost a monster of egotism' and of Annabella as 'virtually a moral defective' is less than just. A more serious flaw in the essay is the use of the plays of Shakespeare's last period as a means of condemning *The Lover's Melancholy*. To say that Ford uses the recognition scene 'on a level hardly higher than that of the device of twins in comedy', that he 'had no conception of what Shakespeare was trying to do' in the recognition scene in *Pericles* and that Ford's scene is 'poetry and drama of the surface' underestimates Ford's understanding of Shakespeare.[18]

In his early criticism Eliot had been too much influenced by the disintegrators, who now seem aberrant, and by Archer's attack on all drama written before Pinero. He had complained that the dramatists were trying to be realistic, yet at the same time he criticized them for departing from colloquial speech. He complained of the lack of recognizable conventions at the very time when Muriel Bradbrook was analysing them. He objected to Lamb's method of anthologizing scenes and speeches while ignoring their contexts; and yet one is bound to remember his own quotations of passages he admired and imitated, rather than his discussion of the dramatic qualities of the plays. He treated them as literature and preferred reading them to seeing them performed. He did, however, lend his approval to productions at the Old Vic; and he once wrote a letter to *The Times*, commending Charles Laughton's performance as Angelo, even though to some of us this was an object lesson in how not to speak Shakespeare's verse.

By 1930, stimulated by his own ambitions as a dramatist, Eliot came to respond more warmly to Shakespeare's plays. He says less about Shakespeare's failings as a purveyor of philosophical commonplaces, and more about the impressiveness of his total *oeuvre* in which each play illuminates the whole and the whole illuminates each play. In particular — perhaps influenced in this by Knight's *Myth and Miracle* and his unpublished *Marina*, which was going the rounds of publishers[19] — Eliot had arrived at a new appreciation of the final plays. Yet his criticism, stimulating as it often is, is not concerned with the theatre; and in this lack of concern, surprising in a dramatist, he has been followed by the best of the *Scrutiny* critics, Leavis, Knights, and Traversi.[20] That is why, when the history of twentieth-century criticism comes to be written objectively, it will be found that the writings of Muriel Bradbrook have ultimately contributed more than Eliot's to our understanding of Elizabethan drama. She has always been concerned with the poets as playwrights, with their relationship with the theatre and the audience — a relationship which may have caused their art to be 'impure', but which was the condition of its greatness.

It may be suggested, finally, that the limitations of Eliot's criticism of Elizabethan drama contributed to the comparative weakness of his own plays. His fear of rhetoric was such that he hoped his audiences would not recognize that his plays were written in verse In the last, and weakest, of the plays, *The Elder Statesman,* he eliminated after the first performance most of the lines and images which might be recognized as 'poetical'.[21] There are two further ironies. In all Eliot's plays, apart from *Sweeney Agonistes,* there are many embarrassing moments, and most of these are due to his uncertainty about conventions. When the Knights in *Murder in the Cathedral* drop into Shavian pastiche, when the uncles and aunts in *The Family Reunion* start declaiming as a chorus, when the Guardians in *The Cocktail Party* sometimes talk like Noël Coward characters, we are hustled from one convention to another. The other irony is that Eliot tried hard to be more and more naturalistic, so that in his last two plays we are not far away from the style of drawing-room comedy and even farce. Eliot's development was similar to the one he deplored in Elizabethan and Jacobean drama.

NOTES

1. Cf. Chapter 2 above.
2. It is significant that the best plays of Masefield, and even of Yeats, are written in prose; and Synge, a better poetic dramatist than either, wrote wholly in prose. In a later essay, 'Poetry and Drama', Eliot spoke enthusiastically of the verse of *Purgatory*, which, he said had put all later poets in Yeats's debt.
3. *Elizabethan Stage Conditions* (Cambridge University Press, 1931); *Themes and Conventions of Elizabethan Tragedy* (Cambridge University Press, 1935).
4. Cf. p. 79 above.
5. The belief that Shakespeare wrote tragedies because of a tragic experience in his own life has a respectable ancestry frm Keats onwards. It was challenged by C. J. Sisson in 'The Mythical Sorrows of Shakespeare' (Oxford University Press, 1934).
6. Cf. Chapter 6 above.
7. See 'Gerontion': 'whirled/Beyond the circuit of the shuddering Bear'.
8. Tourneur's reputation, indeed, depends not on his considerable dramatic powers, but largely on two speeches in his best play — if, indeed, he wrote *The Revenger's Tragedy*.
9. Cf. Kenneth Muir, 'Shakespeare's Use of Rhetoric', *Shakespeare Jahrbuch*, XC (1952), pp. 49-68.
10. See G. K. Hunter, *Dramatic Identities and Cultural Tradition* (Liverpool University Press, 1975), pp. 159-213
11. Ibid., p. 179.
12. Cited by F. O Matthiesen, *The Achievement of T. S. Eliot* (Oxford University Press, 1959), p. 102.
13. Hunter, *op. cit.*, pp. 206 ff.
14. G. Wilson Knight, *The Wheel of Fire* (Oxford University Press, 1930), Introduction.
15. Hunter, *op. cit.*, p. 299.
16. See 'The Role of Livia' in *Poetry and Drama* 1570-1700, ed. Antony Coleman and Antony Hammond (Methuen: London, 1981). Reprinted above.
17. T. S. Eliot, *Collected Poems* (Faber: London, 1963), p. 41:

    > I that was near your heart was removed therefrom
    > To lose beauty in terror, terror in inquisition.
    > I have lost my passion: why should I need to keep it
    > Since what is kept must be adulterated.

18. See above, Chapter 11.

19. See G. Wilson Knight's essay in *Neglected Powers* (Routledge: London, 1971), p. 384.
20. There is a revealing passage by L. C. Knights in 'How Many Children Had Lady Macbeth?' (Reprinted *Explorations,* Chatto and Windus: London 1946). 'How should we read Shakespeare? We start with so many lines of verse on a printed page which we read as we should read any other poem'. It is better, perhaps, to start with an actor on a stage speaking lines to another actor and to an audience.
21. Matthiesen quotes from an unpublished lecture of Eliot's (1933): 'to write poetry which should be essentially poetry, with nothing poetic about it ... poetry so transparent that in reading it we are intent on what the poem *points at,* and not on the poetry'. It may be added that Eliot transferred speeches in the last scene of *The Elder Statesman,* from a male to a female character, and vice versa. Denis Donoghue, *The Third Voice* (Princeton, 1959), is much kinder to the play.

Acknowledgements

My grateful thanks are due to the editors and publishers of the following books and journals:

'Shakespeare's Open Secret' in *Shakespeare Survey* 34 (Cambridge University Press: Cambridge, 1981); 'Shakespeare's Didactic Art', the Pratt Lectureship Committee (St John's Memorial University: St John's, Newfoundland, 1984); 'Folklore and Shakespeare' in *Folklore* (1981); 'The Texts of *King Lear*' in *The Aligarh Journal of English Studies* (1983); 'Theophanies in Shakespeare's Last Plays' in *Shakespeare's Last Plays*, ed. Richard C. Tobias and Paul G. Zolbrod (Ohio University Press: Ohio, 1974); 'Stendhal, Racine and Shakespeare' in *Shakespeare Studies* (1984); 'The Role of Livia' in *Poetry and Drama 1570-1700*, ed. Antony Coleman and Antony Hammond (Methuen: London, 1981); 'Two Plays Reconsidered' in *Accompanying the Players*, ed. Kenneth Friedenreich (AMS Press: 1983); 'The Case of John Ford', first published in *Sewanee Review* 84 (autumn 1976): copyright by the University of the South, 1976; reprinted by permission of the editor; 'T. S. Eliot's Criticism of Elizabethan Drama' in *Mirror up to Shakespeare*, ed. J. C. Gray (University of Toronto Press: Toronto, 1984).

Index